MacClinton

Sam Griffith

To Keith and Stacy —
Pray for America

Sam
Micah 6:8

MacClinton

Sam Griffith

A Parody of MacBeth

The Tragedy of the Clintons

© 2016 by Sam Griffith. All rights reserved.

Published by Conservative Press Books Toll Free (855) 946-2555

Conservative Press Books is an imprint of Redemption Press

No part of this publication may be reproduced, stored in a retrieval system, or transmitted in any way by any means—electronic, mechanical, photocopy, recording, or otherwise—without the prior permission of the copyright holder, except as provided by USA copyright law.

Scripture taken from the New King James Version®. Copyright © 1982 by Thomas Nelson. Used by permission. All rights reserved.

ISBN 13: 978-1-63232-859-5 (SC)
978-1-63232-862-5 (HC)
978-1-63232-865-6 (ePub)
978-1-63232-872-4 (Mobi)

Library of Congress Catalog Card Number: 2015959261

"When the righteous are in authority, the people rejoice; but when a wicked man rules, the people groan" (Proverbs 29:2, New King James Version).

"When a citizen gives his suffrage [vote] to a man of known immorality, he abuses his trust; he sacrifices not only his own interest, but that of his neighbor; he betrays the interest of his country" (Noah Webster).

CONTENTS

Introduction Ix

Main Speaking Cast. Xi

Act One

Scene One 15
Scene Two 17
Scene Three 21
Scene Four 29
Scene Five 31
Scene Six 37
Scene Seven 41

Act Two

Scene One 49
Scene Two 53
Scene Three 57
Scene Four 63

Act Three

Scene One 71
Scene Two 79
Scene Three 83

Act Four

Scene One 89
Scene Two 99
Scene Three 101

Act Five

Scene One 107
Scene Two 111
Scene Three 115
Scene Four 119
Scene Five 121
Scene Six 125
Scene Seven 127

Notes 135
About the Author 173

INTRODUCTION

Bill Clinton's life and career have a lot in common with Shakespeare's play *Macbeth*. Thus *MacClinton* follows the pattern, acts, and scenes of that drama.

In case you've forgotten the play, Macbeth was a thane, or regional ruler under the king of Scotland, King Duncan. Three witches met him and prophesied that he would become the king. Macbeth told his wife about the prophecy, and she urged him to fulfill it.

King Duncan went to Macbeth's castle for a visit, and Lady Macbeth murdered him. Although she washed the king's blood from her hands after her murderous deed, her conscience drove her mad. She was last portrayed in the play as a madwoman, trying vainly to wash the imaginary spots of King Duncan's blood from her hands, lamenting, "Out, damned spot!"

Macbeth became king and violently terrorized and killed his opponents across Scotland, causing some survivors to flee the country. Macbeth was defeated and killed in battle; and King Duncan's son, Malcolm, replaced him.

MacClinton

MacClinton, the Modern Macbeth

In *MacClinton*, the three witches who prophesied Macbeth's future kingship have become three women representing the long line of Clinton's paramours. And, instead of Lady Macbeth trying to wash spots of imaginary blood from her hands, Lady MacClinton is shown moaning, "Out, damned spot!" while trying to wash President Clinton's "spots" off Monica Lewinsky's blue dress.

Instead of King Duncan coming to Macbeth's castle, Senator Bob Dole, the Republican nominee in the 1996 presidential campaign, comes to the Clinton's "castle," the White House.

King Macbeth sent assassins to murder his enemies; and in *MacClinton*, Representative Bob Livingston has his reputation "assassinated." *Macbeth* ends with King Duncan's son, Malcolm, entering the castle, proclaiming his reign, calling his followers lords of the kingdom, and calling for a banquet. *MacClinton* ends as Texas Governor George W. Bush enters the White House as the newly elected President of the United States, proclaiming his followers to be "honorary Texas Rangers" and calling for a barbeque.

The Clinton Tragedy

Bill and Hillary Clinton's careers are rife with scandals, to which *MacClinton* attests. Summaries of many of them are in the Notes section.

Although *MacClinton* is a parody of the Clinton administration, for the American people his administration was a tragedy.

MAIN SPEAKING CAST

(See Notes for more information.)

*ITCHES: representatives of Bill Clinton's extramarital paramours

GOVERNOR BUSH: George W. Bush, governor of Texas, forty-third President of the United States and Bill Clinton's successor

LADY MACCLINTON: Hillary Clinton, Bill's wife

LADY MACWILLEY: Kathleen Willey, a White House volunteer aide who alleged President Bill Clinton sexually assaulted her

LADY MACSTARR: Alice Starr, wife of Ken Starr who investigated allegations of Bill Clinton's affair with Monica Lewinsky

MACARMEY: Dick Armey, Republican House Majority Leader who co-authored the Contract with America pledge

MacClinton

that resulted in a Republican majority in both the House and Senate in the 1994 election

MACCLINTON: William Jefferson "Bill" Clinton, forty-second President of the United States and former governor of Arkansas

MACDELAY: Tom DeLay, Republican Congressional leader led the Republican dominated U.S. House of Representatives in 1998 to enact legislation which produced the first balanced budget since 1969.

MACDOLE: Robert "Bob" Dole, Republican Senator from Kansas and 1996 Republican nominee for President against Bill Clinton

MACFILE: Craig Livingstone, the Clinton White House's director of personnel security who improperly requested FBI documents

MACGINGRICH: Newt Gingrich, Republican Speaker of the House of Representatives who co-authored the Contract with America pledge that resulted in a Republican majority in both the House and Senate in the 1994 election

MACHYDE: Henry Hyde, a Republican House leader in President Clinton's impeachment trial

MACLIVINGSTON: Robert Livingston, U.S. Representative who resigned from Congress for a past affair, calling on President Clinton to follow his example

MACSTARR: Kenneth Starr, lawyer and former federal judge who was appointed independent counsel to investigate the suicide of Vince Foster, the Clintons' Whitewater real-estate investments, and allegations of Bill Clinton's affair with Monica Lewinsky

MONICA: Monica Lewinsky, a White House intern who had an affair with President Bill Clinton

ACT ONE

SCENE ONE

(Setting: lingerie aisle of a department store during a blue-light special[1] with a blue, turning light on a pole and a distant voice announcing on a microphone, "Women's fashion bras are half off for the next fifteen minutes."

Enter three *itches, who are obviously peroxide blondes with high, bouffant hairdos and large, silicone-enhanced chests, wearing lots of make-up and tight stretch clothes. One has a strong nose. They speak with Arkansas twangs as they peruse the merchandise, holding up various items and putting them back.)

*ITCH 1: When shall we three meet again
    In thunder, lightning or in rain,
    In the district court,
    Or on David Letterman? *(She laughs, her voice almost a cackle.)*

*ITCH 2: When the hurlyburly's done,
    When the court battles are lost and won.

MacClinton

*ITCH 3: Or likely before the setting of the sun.

*ITCH 1: Where the place?

*ITCH 2: At the motel at the edge of town.

(*Background music plays: The Amazing Rhythm Aces's "Third Rate Romance, Low-Rent Rendezvous."*)

*ITCH 3: There to meet with MacClinton.[2]

*ITCHES 1-3: (*Cackle with laughter.*) Again! (*Cackle with laughter again.*)

LITTLE GIRL (*yelling from next aisle over, dragging out the syllables*): Mama.

*ITCH 1: I'm comin', my Kathryn.

OLDER MAN (*growling voice from next aisle over*): Betty Jean?

*ITCH 2: Daddy calls. (*yelling*) In a minute.

(*in speaking voice to other women*): What do ya'll think about the new chicken processing plant south of town?[3]

*ITCH 3: The stench is fowl,

But the wage is fair.

*ITCHES 1-3: Fair is fair, and fowl are foul.

The stench of wet chickens

Hovers through the fog and filthy air.

(*They separate, pushing their shopping carts down the aisles and laughing.*)

Scene Two

(*Setting: Camp David. A high-powered office with elaborate desk; credenza; fax machine; telephones with multiple lines; and a grouping of a couch, overstuffed chairs, end tables, and coffee table. An aide sits behind the desk, talking on the phone.*

Enter MacClinton; Lawyer; White House Aide, who is thin-faced and pale with black, wire-rimmed glasses; a herd of aides and sycophants; a group of powerful-acting, high-dollar lawyers with expensive suits, briefcases, laptop computers, and buzzing cell phones.)

WHITE HOUSE AIDE: Got to go. Bye. (*He hangs up the phone, then leaps to his feet.*)
 Mr. MacClinton! Sir! Can I get you anything?

(*The wave of lawyers and aides wash him away. The lawyers spread out, set their laptops on the desk and credenza, and open their briefcases. Several obvious leaders follow and huddle around MacClinton. Enter Stunned Lawyer.*)

MacClinton

MacClinton: Lawyer?
>What bloody man is that? He can impart,
>As seen by his plight of the court,
>Of its latest report.

Lawyer: This is the trial lawyer,
>Who like a good soldier has fought
>'Gainst your enemies. Hail, brave friend!

(Lawyer and Stunned Lawyer shake hands.)
>Say to the President your knowledge of the court
>When you did leave it.

Stunned Lawyer: Doubtful it stood.
>As two spent swimmers that cling together
>And choke their art, so clutched together the lawyers. MacStarr,[1]
>He is worthy to be a cigarette lawyer,[2] for to that
>The multiplying villainies of nature
>Do swarm upon him from the Western and Southern states.
>A vast right-wing conspiracy[3] is supplied;
>And Fortune, on his damned face smiling,
>Showed who he favored; but all's too weak.
>The knave MacStarr—well he deserves that name—
>Disdaining tobacco's fortune,[4] with his brandished steel,
>Which smoked with bloody execution,
>Like Valhalla's minion, carved out his passage
>'Til he faced the grave,
>The dour MacDougals.[5]
>He ne'er shook hands,

Act One - Scene Two

    Nor bade farewell to him,
    Until he unseamed Jim,
    From his navy blazer
    To his pork chops.
    And fixed Jim's head upon his conviction lists.
WHITE HOUSE AIDE: God save us all.
LAWYER *(to Stunned Lawyer)*: O, valiant nephew!
    (aside to MacClinton): He's married to my niece, you know.
    (aloud): Worthy gentleman!
CAMPAIGN AIDE: Damn that Reno![6]
    But for her weakness
    MacStarr would been a no-go!
    No sooner the Justice Department had, with valor armed,
    Compelled these nipping GOP worms to trust their heels,
    And leave our '96 victory alone,[7]
    But the vast right-wing lords, surveying their vantage,
    Did furnish bank accounts and new supplies of men,
    Began a fresh assault.
MACCLINTON: Dismayed not this
    Our lawyers?
LAWYER: Yes,
    As sparrows, eagles, or the hare, the lion,
    As the donkey,[8] the . . . *(pauses as he thinks)* the, uh . . .
    (aside to Stunned Lawyer): Pull yourself together, Boy.
    (to MacClinton): If I say truth, I must report they were
    As cannons overcharged with double cracks,

MacClinton

> We've got to doubly redouble our strokes upon the Republican foe.
> They mean to bathe again, in reeking wounds,
> Our dear, departed MacFoster,[9]
> Or memorialize another Golgotha![10]
> The Whitewater[11] surges against us
> As we await the fall of the next nut from your native forest,[12] sir.

CAMPAIGN AIDE: Just have to drag an acorn through a Whitewater forest parking lot,[13]
> And watch the forest trash that doth appear,
> To attack and bark, and sue for cash so dear!

STUNNED LAWYER: I cannot tell.
> But I am faint, my trial briefs cry for help.

MACCLINTON: So well thy words become thee, as thy courtroom wounds
> Smack of honor both. Go, get him to the law library.

(Exit Stunned Lawyer.)

SCENE THREE

(*Setting: cheap motel parking lot. Three vehicles are parked close together: a green, mid-1960s Mustang; an early 1970s El Camino pickup with Astroturf in the back;[1] and a worn, late 1970s Cadillac DeVille. The three blonde *itches are talking and lounging against the Cadillac, wearing lots of makeup and tight, low-cut dresses. Each woman is carrying a small overnight case. Above and behind them, the last leg of the M on the red neon MOTEL sign is unlit, so the sign reads NOTEL (no-tell motel). In smaller letters, a green neon sign proclaims "Vacancies."*

A clap of thunder. The three women jump and look up.)

*ITCH 1: Where hast thou been, Sister?

*ITCH 2: Killing swine.

*ITCH 3: Say it, Sister. Where, who?

*ITCH 2: MacClinton, that pig!
    He thinks he's the master of the tiger.
    But I swear,

MacClinton

      I'll put his tail in a crack,
      And then he'll be like a rat without a tail.
      I'll do it, I'll do it, I'll do it!
*ITCH 3: What happened?
*ITCH 2: MacClinton's wife, the big ham!
      She recognized me from the party
      Last Christmas when MacClinton
      And I came out of the coatroom
      With my lipstick smeared.[2]

(They all break into laughter and nudge one another.)

*ITCH 2 *(spitting the words with venom)*: She called me trailer trash!

(The others recoil as if slapped when they hear these words.)

*ITCH 1: What have you done, Sister?
*ITCH 2: I've been to see the king slayer, MacStarr.[3]
      I've told him the secrets that I have learned,
      About MacClinton from his own man.
*ITCH 3: You mean . . . *(pauses, then smiles broadly)*
*ITCH 2 *(nodding her head)*: Yep.
*ITCH 3: Morris, that Dick,[4]
      What a talker.

(They all laugh.)

*ITCH 2: I will drain him dry as hay.
      He'll sleep neither night nor day

Act One - Scene Three

And hand upon his penthouse lid,
He shall live a man forbid.
Weary though nights nine times nine
Shall he dwindle, peak, and pine.
Though his office cannot be lost,
For Democrats will back him at any cost,[5]
Yet it shall be tempest-tost.

*ITCH 1: I'll give him my middle thumb,
Wrecked as homeward he does come. *(She holds her middle finger up in the air.)*

(A car horn blows.)

*ITCH 3: A car. It is him!
MacClinton has come.
*ITCHES 1-3: The weird sisters, hand in hand,
Poster girls of the sea and land,
Thus do go, about, about,
Thrice to thine, and thrice to mine,
And thrice again, to make up nine.
Peace! *(They all make the peace sign toward the approaching car.)*
Our charms wound up.

(The women throw out their ample chests and pose coquettishly, batting their big eyelashes at the approaching car. Enter a black limousine with the presidential seal on the door and a license-plate frame that says "Arkansas is for lovers." It stops next to the three women. A darkly tinted back-door window glides down. MacClinton is in the back seat, lustfully evaluating the selection for his evening's pleasure. The driver, seen through

MacClinton

the untinted driver's window, is smirking as MacClinton makes his move.)

MACCLINTON: So fowl and fair a day I have not seen.
    That chicken plant stinks, if you know what I mean.
    (to the driver): Who are these,
    So witchy, and so wild in their attire,
    They look not like the inhabitants o' DC
    (to the women): You girls want to live it up?

(The women do not answer but pose more provocatively.)

    Are you aught that man may question?
    You seem to understand me,
    But each at once, lay your cute lips on me.[6]
    You be some sexy women.
    Speak, if you can. Who are you?
*ITCH 1: All hail MacClinton! Hail to the chief![7]
*ITCH 2: All hail MacClinton! Hail to the chief!
*ITCH 3: All hail MacClinton! Hail to the chief!
DRIVER *(to MacClinton):* Good sir, why do you start, and seem to fear
    Things that do sound so fair? In the name of truth,
    Are ye fantastical, or that indeed, so horny[8] to want these
    Which outwardly show you their wares.
    (lowers his window and speaks to the women): You greet us with present grace,
    And I have a great prediction:
    You of noble having and of a royal hope,
    That he seems rapt with you all.

Act One - Scene Three

But you speak not to me, you stuck-up wenches,
If you can look into the seeds of time,
And say which grain will grow and which will not,
Speak then to me, who neither begs nor fears
Your favors nor your hate.

*ITCH 1: Hail to Bill!
*ITCH 2: Hail to Bill!
*ITCH 3: Hail to Bill!

(They cluster close to the driver's window and speak to the driver.)

*ITCH 1: Lesser than MacClinton, and greater.
*ITCH 2: Not so happy, yet much happier.[9]
*ITCH 3: Thou shalt get kings, though thou be none.
*ITCHES 1-3: But to hell with you tonight.

(They move back and cluster by MacClinton's open rear window.)

MACCLINTON: Stay here, you imperfect sweet thangs, tell me more.

(The women cluster closer to MacClinton's window with more provocative poses and giggle loudly.)

Say from whence
You owe this strange intelligence, or why
Upon this blasted Arkansas parking lot, you stop our way

MacClinton

>With such a propositional greeting? Speak, I charge
>you.

*(He opens the door and slides over. The three women vanish
into the car with him, the door closes, and the car leaves.)*

MACCLINTON *(leaning forward and talking quietly to the
driver):* Take us to that trusted home,
>My home away from home[10]
>Where these ladies
>Might yet enkindle and light my flame,
>But it is strange, you know,
>Oftentimes, to win us to our harm,
>The instruments of darkness tell us truths,[11]
>Win us with honest trifles, to betray us
>In deepest consequence.
>Cousin, not a word I pray you, to my missus. *(pats a
>bare thigh)*
>Two truths are told,
>As happy prologues to the swelling act
>Of the imperial theme.
>As Julius Caesar said,
>"I came. I saw. I conquered."
>*(he pauses as he ponders the phrase, and the order of the
>three statements)*
>Or is that in the right order for tonight?

(They laugh.)

>Besides, all this supernatural soliciting
>Cannot be ill;

Act One - Scene Three

> But three at one time cannot be good. If ill,
> Why hath it given me promise of success,
> And make my seated heart knock at my ribs,
> Against the use of nature? Present fears of discovery
> Are less than horrible imaginings of my wife if she finds out.
> My thought of my murder[12] yet is but fantastical,
> So shakes my single state of man that function
> Is smothered in surmise, and nothing is
> But what is not.

DRIVER *(turning suddenly to look back over the seat):* Huh?

MACCLINTON: If chance will have me President, why
> chance may crown me three times tonight,
> Without my stir.
> Come what come may,
> Time and the hour runs through the roughest day.
> Driver, to a hidden hideaway,
> Without making any delay.

(MacClinton sits back in his seat and is covered by the women who are smothering him with hugs and kisses.)

SCENE FOUR

(Setting: hidden hideaway motel. MacClinton, the three *itches, and the driver enter the front door. MacClinton is hugging, clutching, and kissing the three blondes; and the women are hugging and kissing MacClinton. The driver is carrying the women's overnight bags. The elderly couple behind the check-in desk look uncomfortable as the driver completes the sign-in sheet.)

DRIVER *(turning to MacClinton)*: All done, Boss.
> *(He tosses a room key to one of the blondes, who catches it in midair and then shakes it like a toy bone in front of MacClinton's face. He bites at it. As a group, they all head down the hall to the room, still snuggling and hugging.)*

OLD WOMAN *(looking disgustedly at the group as they leave)*:
> To throw away the dearest thing he owned
> As 'twere a careless trifle,
> On three worthless trifles.

MacClinton

OLD MAN *(shaking his head slowly):* There's no art
    To find the mind's construction in the face.
    He was a gentleman on whom I built
    An absolute trust.[1]

(He takes down a "MacClinton for President" poster behind the counter, tears it up, and tosses it in the trash with a sigh.)

    For such actions, there's the Devil to pay
    Only this I have to say,
    More is thy due
    Than more than all can pay.

SCENE FIVE

(Setting: Lady MacClinton's White house office. Enter Lady MacClinton, holding a fax from MacClinton.)

LADY MACCLINTON *(reading from the fax):*
>I met with the reporters after a successful day of campaigning;
>And I have learned from past experience and their report
>They have more in them than mortal knowledge.
>When they burned in desire to question me further,[1]
>I made myself thin air, into which I vanished.
>While I stood rapt in wonder of the manipulation of a compliant press,[2]
>Came missives from the polls who all-hailed me,
>"Reelected President,"
>By which title, before,
>I have been saluted of late,

MacClinton

    And referred to me to the coming on of time,
    With "Hail to the Chief." That shall be mine!
    This have I thought good to deliver thee,
    My dearest partner of greatness,
    That thou mightest not lose the dues of rejoicing,
    By being ignorant of what greatness is promised me
    And thus to thee.
    Lay it to thy heart, and farewell.
    Oh, I won't be home 'til late tonight.
    Forgive me, and don't let the bedbugs bite.

(She wads the fax into a tight roll, then twists it as if strangling someone with a vengeance.)

    "I won't be home 'til late tonight."
    Yeah, right!
    What floozy is it tonight?
    That bastard! Forgive him, hell.
    When it comes to the milk of human kindness, I'm
        lactose intolerant.[3]
    If I find out who this tramp is
    I'll sic the FBI[4] on her so quick it'll make her empty
        head swim.
    Come, you spirits[5]
    That tend on mortal thoughts, unsex me here,
    And fill me from the crown to the toe top-full
    Of direst cruelty! Make thick my blood;
    Stop up the access and passage of remorse,
    That no compunctious visitings of nature
    Shake my fell purpose, nor keep peace between
    The effect and it! Come to my woman's breasts,

Act One - Scene Five

> And take my milk for gall, you murdering ministers
> Wherever in your sightless substances
> You wait on nature's mischief! Come, thick night,
> And pall thee in the darkest smoke of hell,
> That my keen knife see not the wound it makes,
> Nor heaven peep through the blanket of the dark,
> To cry "Hold, hold!"

(She picks up the telephone and punches in a number, then rests it under her chin and waits for it to be answered, impatiently tapping on the phone with a pen. When the phone is answered, she speaks into it with a rich, lustful voice, low and soothing, to someone she obviously knows well.)

> He won't be home again tonight.
> Is the disappearance of the records[6] going right?
> You've got to separate me from those
> Land and bank records of note. *(pauses, then says sharply)*
> Well, hurry it up.
> If it were done, when 'tis done,
> Then 'twere well it were done quickly.

She hangs up the phone sharply, then wanders around the room, deep in thought, musing aloud to herself.

> If this shredding could trammel up the consequence, and catch,
> With his surcease, success; that but this blow
> Might be the be-all and the end-all here,
> But here, upon this bank and shoal of time,

MacClinton

> We'd jump the life to come. But in these cases
> We still have judgment here. That we but teach
> Bloody instructions, which being taught return
> To plague the inventor. This evenhanded justice
> Commends the ingredients of our poisoned chalice
> To our own lips. He's here in double trust,
> Thereby achieve success,
> Then let this shredding be the be-all and the end-all.
> *(pauses)*
> Damn, we're so close to success
> And yet a sea of documents can drown us
> And cause us to lose the White House.
> So many people working so hard for us.
> We have sent the FBI and IRS
> To harass our enemies,
> Enemies in the Travel Office,[7]
> Enemies in Congress,
> Enemies in the media. *(pauses)*
> I wonder what Richard Nixon[8] would say, though?
> That we always have our judgment here,
> That which we teach, being taught, returns to plague the inventor?[9]
> Maybe I'll have my psychic channel Nixon tonight
> And talk with his ghost, rather than Eleanor Roosevelt.

(She picks up a letter opener and, eying its edge carefully, runs her finger along the blade.)

> But what can we do? What can we do? What would Lorena Bobbitt[10] do?

Act One - Scene Five

(Her face displays indecision, then her jaw sets as she makes a decision. She stabs the desk with the letter opener, leaving it sticking up in the wood.)

(Enter MacClinton.)

LADY MACCLINTON: Great Gatsby's Ghost! What are you doing here?
    Greater than President George H. W. Bush! Greater than Bob MacDole!
    Greater than both, by all that hail us hereafter!
    Your letters have transported me beyond
    This ignorant present, and I feel now
    The future is in the instant.

MACCLINTON: That's what Gore keeps saying, "The future is now!"
    Anywho, my dearest love,
    Senator Bob MacDole comes here tonight for a state dinner.

LADY MACCLINTON: And when goes he hence?

MACCLINTON: Tomorrow, as he purposes to campaign in California.

LADY MACCLINTON: O, never
    Shall sun that morrow see
    That that Republican will carry Californi-e.
    Your face, my love, is as a book where men
    May read strange matters. To beguile the press,
    Look like old times. Bear welcome in your eye.
    Your hand, your tongue look like the innocent flower,[11]
    But I'll be the serpent under it. He that's coming
    Must be provided for and you shall put

MacClinton

 This night's great business into my hands,
 Which shall to all our nights and days to come.
 Give sovereign sway and masterdom,
 And we'll be co-President[12] 'til the millennium come.

MacClinton: We will speak further tonight.
Lady MacClinton: You look the press in the eyes,
 And tell them more of your fluid lies.
 Leave all the rest to me.

Scene Six

(Setting: a White House room. Enter MacDole and several Senate aides.)

MacDole *(speaking in flat, Kansas accent)*: This house sits in a pleasant location; the air
    Nimbly and sweetly recommends itself
    Unto our senses. Bob MacDole likes it.[1]
    Bob MacDole likes being on this end of Pennsylvania Avenue.[2]

Senate Aide *(pointing to a bird's nest)*: This guest of summer,
    The church-haunting starling, does approve,
    And he loves this place, the heaven's breath
    Smells wooingly here. There is no corner of this White House
    But that this bird
    Hath made his nests
    Where they most breed and haunt, I have observed
    The air is delicate.

MacClinton

MacDole: Bob MacDole likes birds.
> We had birds in Kansas. Bob MacDole likes Kansas and birds.
> Elizabeth likes birds. Bob MacDole really likes Elizabeth.[3]

(Enter Lady MacClinton.)

MacDole *(aside to aide, glaring at Lady MacClinton):* But Bob MacDole doesn't like her!
> *(aloud to Lady MacClinton):* See, see! Our honored hostess!
> The voters' love that follow us sometime is our trouble,
> But still we appreciate their love.
> And thank you for your trouble of inviting us.

Lady MacClinton: All our service
> If twice done and then done double,
> Is poor repayment for your gracious presence
> Against your honors deep and broad, wherewith
> Your presence brings to our house. We are honored.

MacDole: Where's the President?
> We thought we'd beat him here from Ronald Reagan Airport;
> But he rides well. His limousine beat us to the gate,
> And his great love, which is sharp as his spur—
> Not to mention the ten-car police escort—helps get him
> To his home before us. Fair and noble hostess,
> We are your guests tonight.

Act One – Scene Six

LADY MACCLINTON: Our servants ever
>Have their place themselves, and what is theirs, is ours, and yours
>
>For your highest pleasure,
>
>'Til you return to your own
>
>*(under her breath):* End of Pennsylvania Avenue.
>
>Give me your hand. Oops, wrong hand.[4] Sorry.

MACDOLE: Bob MacDole gave his body, almost his life, in the service of his country.[5] Bob MacDole is a patriot. Bob MacDole is a public servant.

LADY MACCLINTON: Let me conduct you to your host; we love him highly,
>And shall continue our graces toward him.

(Exit all.)

SCENE SEVEN

(Setting: a room in the White House presidential quarters. Enter MacClinton with his head down and shoulders hunched like he's trying to avoid a tongue lashing. Right behind him enters Lady MacClinton.)

LADY MACCLINTON: How goes the Paula Jones, trailer-trash, bimbo-eruption smear campaign?

MACCLINTON: If it were done, when 'tis done, then 'twere well
It were done quickly. If the character assassination
Could trammel up the consequence, and catch,
With her destruction, success; but that this blow
Might be the be-all and the end-all here,
To this squalid mess.
But here, upon this bank and shoal of time,
We'd jump the life to come.
But in these sexual-harassment cases
We still have judgments here; that we but teach

MacClinton

> Bloody instructions, which being taught return
> To plague the inventor. This evenhanded justice
> Commends the ingredients of our poisoned chalice
> To our own lips.
> It's not fair!
> By destroying others, our legacy ends up tarnished.
> I thought we'd been packing the federal courts with our lackeys.[1]
> Where's a lackey when you need one?

LADY MACCLINTON: What about Senator MacDole?
> He's downstairs for a state dinner. How are we going to destroy him?

MACCLINTON: He's here in double trust.
> First he's an honored veteran and statesman,
> Argue against the deed. Then, as his host,
> Who should against his destroyer shut the door,
> Not bear the knife myself.
> Besides, isn't that what the campaign spokesmen are for?
> Anyway, MacDole hath borne his faculties so meek,
> Hath borne his great office so well, that his virtues
> Will plead like angels, trumpet-tongued, against
> The deep damnation of his destruction;
> And pity, like a naked newborn babe,
> Or Heaven's cherubim, horsed
> Upon the winds of the air,
> Shall blow the horrid deed in every eye,
> That tears shall drown the wind.
> I would "feel his pain"[2] if we destroyed him.

Act One - Scene Seven

LADY MACCLINTON: Good line. I like it. Hell, even I almost believe you.
>Like I said earlier, you are an innocent flower when you turn on the BS.
>Now, see if you can tear up just a little.
>Those soccer moms[3] really eat up that "I feel your pain" BS.

MACCLINTON: I have no spur to prick the sides of my intent, but only
>Vaulting ambition, which o'erleaps itself,
>And falls on the other side.

LADY MACCLINTON: You want something to spur your ambition?
>*(yelling)* Let me tell you, I'll make your life a living hell if you don't get after it.
>Is that "spur" enough for you?

MACCLINTON *(head down)*: Yes, Dear.

LADY MACCLINTON *(mocking, singsong voice)*: "My partner in greatness" my ass.
>I've carried you to these heights
>And you won't quit on me now.

MACCLINTON: Yes, Dear.

LADY MACCLINTON: And another thing . . .

(White House aide enters.)

>How now! What news?

WHITE HOUSE AIDE: He has almost supped. He asked why you two left the East Wing.

MacClinton

MACCLINTON: Has he asked for me?
LADY MACCLINTON: You know he has.
    (*to aide*) Tell them we'll be there soon.
MACCLINTON: We will proceed no further in this business.
    I have been honored of late, and I bought,
    Thank goodness for that red Chinese fundraising junket,[4]
    Golden opinions from all sorts of people,
    Which should be worn now in their newest gloss,
    Not cast aside so soon.
LADY MACCLINTON: Was hope drunk
    Wherein you dressed yourself? Hath it slept since?
    And wakes it now, to look so green and pale
    At what it did so freely? From this time
    Such I account thy love. Art thou afeard
    To be the same in thine own act and valor
    As thou art in desire? Would you have stolen that
    Which you have esteemed as the ornament of life,
    And live a coward in your own esteem,
    Letting "I dare not" wait upon "I would?"
MACCLINTON: Pray thee, peace, woman.
    I dare do all that may become a man;
    Who dares do more is none.
LADY MACCLINTON: You and your "man" issues!
    Making it with every slut this side of the Pacific Ocean
    Does *not* "become a man," nor do you become a man by doing them!
    I'm warning you, Bill, one more bimbo,
    And I'll hire Lorena Bobbitt for your next White House intern!

Act One - Scene Seven

>What beast was it then
>That made you break this enterprise to me?
>We had great plans for this presidency.
>When you dared do it, then you were a man;
>And, to be more than what you were, you would
>Be so much more the man. Neither time nor place
>Did then adhere, and yet you would make both.
>They have made themselves, and that their fitness now
>Does unmake you. I have given suck, and know
>How tender 'tis to love the babe that milks me.
>I would, while it was smiling in my face,
>Have plucked my nipple from her boneless gums,
>And dashed the brains out, had I so sworn as you
>Have done to this.

MACCLINTON: If we should fail?

LADY MACCLINTON: We fail?
>But screw your courage to the sticking place,
>And we'll fail not.
>We'll follow through on the "bimbo eruption" smear campaign,
>So that will take care of those problems.[5]
>If you will just promise to keep your "wee willie" home for a while,
>We won't have any more problems,
>And those problems will be zipped up. OK?
>The Whitewater documents are no more.
>And tonight at dinner, smile at MacDole, be friendly,
>And while MacDole bores the audience to sleep,
>We'll squish him in the polls.

MacClinton

MACCLINTON: Bring forth men-children only!
>   For thy undaunted mettle should compose
>   Nothing but males. *You* do all that becomes a man.
>   *You the man,* Hillary!
>   Anyway, who will believe those women
>   When we have bloodied those women's reputations,
>   And used their very daggers, their character?
>   Who will believe that I've done it?

LADY MACCLINTON: Who would dare interpret it otherwise,
>   As we shall make our griefs and clamor roar
>   Upon the death of the women's liberation movement.[6]

MACCLINTON: OK, you've sold me. I am settled, and am ready
>   To use every corporal agent to this terrible feat.
>   Maybe we can get some FBI files on some of these women?
>   Or have the IRS investigate them?[7] That'll keep them busy!
>   What's the use of running a government,
>   If you can't run down your enemies with it?
>   OK, Honeybunch, let's go and have dinner,
>   And make with the fairest show,
>   False face to hide what the false heart doth know.

LADY MACCLINTON: We both know what slippery slime you are when you try, Bill.
>   I've never been prouder of you. I'll try to put on a happy face. *(pauses)*
>   But I'm warning you: One more affair and I'll divorce you
>   And I'll get Chelsea and this House in the divorce decree!

(Exit all. Curtain.)

Act Two

SCENE ONE

(Setting: White House hallway. Enter three White house aides, Tom, Dick, and Harry. Harry carries a folder.)

DICK: How goes the night, Boy?

TOM: The moon is down;
    I have not heard the clock.

DICK: And she goes down at seven.

TOM: I take it, 'tis later, sir.

HARRY: Hold up, here, take my press folder.
    There's husbandry in heaven,
    Their candles are all out.
    A heavy grand jury summons lies like lead on me,
    And yet I would not sleep. Merciful powers,
    Restrain in me the cursed thoughts that nature
    Gives way in repose! Give me back my files.

MacClinton

>The nightmares of more bimbo eruptions disturb my sleep.
>Who's there?

(Enter MacClinton and the darkened image of a woman in the shadows, slipping through the door of a side office. The three men's eyes follow the woman and, with slumping shoulders, face MacClinton.)

MACCLINTON: She's just a friend. Don't tell Hillary, OK?

DICK: Uh, er, sure. What, sir, you're not yet at rest? The queen's a-bed.
>She has been in unusual pleasure,
>Because the Chinese have
>Sent forth great largess to your offices.[1]
>This diamond they greet your wife with,
>Because she was such a kind hostess,
>Maybe now they will shut up Charlie Trie's grand jury testimony,[2]
>In measureless content.
>So all is well.
>I dreamt last night of the three weird sisters.
>You told me about them often enough,
>And I can't get them out of my mind.
>To you they have showed some truth.

MACCLINTON: I think not of them.
>Yet, when we can entreat an hour to spare,
>We would spend it in some words upon that business,
>If you would grant me the time.
>And then I'll tell you about the two sets of twins I met
>In California last month.

Act Two - Scene One

DICK: At your kindest leisure. *(rubs his forehead like he's getting a headache)*

MACCLINTON *(leaning toward Dick and speaking quietly)*:
    If you shall cleave to my defense when needed,
    I'll make honor for you.

DICK: As long as I lose none
    In your seeking to augment your story, but if I can keep
    My bosom uncalled and allegiance clear,
    You know I shall be counseled,
    I have a great criminal defense lawyer.

MACCLINTON: Good repose the while. Don't let the bed bugs bite.

(He waves over his shoulder as he strolls back toward the door where the woman disappeared.)

TOM: Thanks, sir, the same to you!
    It's *his* bedbugs that keep biting us in the ass. Bimbo eruptions, indeed.

Scene Two

(Setting: Oval Office. MacClinton is seated behind his desk, deep in thought, when suddenly he startles at the silhouette of Monica wearing a beret.[1])

MacClinton: Is this a thong underwear[2] which I see before me,
    The hind toward my hand? Come, let me clutch thee.
    I have thee not, and yet I see thee still.
    Art thou not, fatal vision, sensible
    To feeling as to sight? Or art thou but
    A dagger of the mind, a false creation,
    Proceeding from the heat-oppressed brain?
    I see thee yet, in form as palpable
    As this cigar[3] which now I hold.
    Thou pointest me the way that I was going, *(holds up the cigar)*
    And such an instrument I was to use!

MacClinton

>Mine eyes are made the fools of the other senses,
>Or else, worth all the rest. I see thee still;
>And on thy backside there are spots,
>Which were not there before. There's no such thing.
>It is the bloody business which informs
>Thus to my eyes. Now o'er the one half-word
>Nature seems dead, and wicked dreams abuse
>The curtained sleep; now witchcraft celebrates
>Pale goddess Monica's off'rings.

(*Woman in silhouette giggles.*)

>And character assassination,[4]
>Led by his sentinel, the wolf,
>Who howls his watch, thus with his stealthy pace,
>With his ravishing strides, toward his designs,
>Moves like a ghost.

WOMAN IN SILHOUETTE: Oh, Bill, you sure do talk funny sometimes.
>Bill, you really do love me, don't you?
>This isn't just sex, is it?[5]

MACCLINTON: Would I lie to you, Sweet Thang?
>Com'mere now. Give me a hug.

(*They embrace, then the telephone rings. MacClinton picks up the phone and puts his hand over it.*)

>Don't stop now, Baby.[6]
>Be sure and firm-set earth,
>Hear not my steps, which way they walk, for fear

Act Two - Scene Two

>   Thy very stones tell of my whereabouts,
>   And take the present horrors from *The Times*,
>   And sells it to *The National Enquirer*.
>   While I threaten, he lives.
>   Words to the heat of deeds too cold breath gives.

WOMAN IN SILHOUETTE: Huh? What do you mean?

MACCLINTON: Too much talking, and not enough action.
>   *(listens to the phone.)* Hi. OK, sounds good. OK. *(hangs up the phone)*
>   They go, and it is done; the bell invited me.
>   Hear it not, Bob Livingston,[7] for it is a knell
>   That summons thee to heaven? Nah, mass media hell.[8]
>   Honeybunch, that feels so-o-o good.

WOMAN IN SILHOUETTE: Does willie want to come out and play?

(The lights go out.)

Scene Three

(Setting: a room in the White House presidential quarters. Lady MacClinton enters.)

LADY MACCLINTON: That which hath made them drunk hath made me bold.
    What hath quenched them hath given me fire. Hark! Peace!
    It was the owl that shrieked, the fatal bellman,
    Which gives the sternest good-night. He is about it.
    The doors are open, and the drunken Republican PR men
    Do mock their charge with snores. I have drugged their drinks,
    That death and nature do contend about them,
    Whether they live or die.
    (MacClinton, from off stage) Who's there? What, ho!
    Alack! I am afraid they have awaked,

MacClinton

> And 'tis not done. The attempt and not the deed
> Confounds us. Hark! I laid their FBI files ready,[1]
> He could not miss 'em. Had he not resembled
> My father, I had done it.

(Enter MacClinton.)

> My husband!

MacClinton: I have done the deed. Didst thou not hear a noise?

Lady MacClinton: I heard the owl scream and the crickets cry. Did you not speak?

MacClinton: When?

Lady MacClinton: Now.

MacClinton: As I descended?

Lady MacClinton: Ay.

MacClinton: Hark! Who lies in the second chamber?

Lady MacClinton: Senator Lott.[2]

MacClinton: This is a sorry sight.

Lady MacClinton: A foolish thought, to say a sorry sight.

MacClinton: There's one did laugh in his sleep, and one cried, "Murder!"
> That they did wake each other; I stood and heard them
> But they did say their prayers, and addressed them
> Again to sleep.

Lady MacClinton: There are two lodged together.

MacClinton: One cried, "God bless us!" and "Amen" the other,

> As they had seen me with these hangman's hands.
> List'ning their fear, I could not say, "Amen,"
> When they did say, "God bless us."

LADY MACCLINTON: Consider it not so deeply,
> For what difference at this point does it make?[3]

MACCLINTON: But wherefore could not I pronounce "Amen?"
> I had most need of blessing, and "Amen"
> Stuck in my throat.

LADY MACCLINTON: These deeds must not be thought
> After these ways; so, it will make us mad.

MACCLINTON: Methought I heard a voice say, "Sleep no more!
> MacClinton does murder sleep," the innocent sleep,
> Sleep that knits up the raveled sleeve of care,
> The death of each day's life, sore labor's bath,
> Balm of hurt minds, great nature's second course,
> Chief nourisher in life's feast,

LADY MACCLINTON: What do you mean?

MACCLINTON: Still it cried, "Sleep no more!" to all the House.[4]
> "MacClinton hath murdered sleep, and therefore MacClinton
> Shall sleep no more. MacClinton shall sleep no more!"

LADY MACCLINTON: Who was it that thus cried? Why, worthy thane,
> You do unbend your noble strength, to think
> So brainsickly of things.
> Why did you bring this cigar and this blue dress[5] from the place?
> Thy must lie there; go carry them away. Go get some water,

MacClinton

>And wash this filthy witness from this dress.⁶

MacClinton: I'll go no more.
>I am afraid to think what I have done;
>To look on it again I dare not.

Lady MacClinton: Infirm of purpose!
>Give me the cigars. The sleeping and the dead
>Are but as pictures, 'tis the eye of childhood
>That fears a painted devil. If he does bleed,
>I'll gild the faces of the grooms withal,
>For it must seem their guilt for not protecting him.
>*(Exits.)*

(Knocking within. MacClinton goes to the bathroom door.)

MacClinton: Whence is that knocking?
>How is it with me, when every noise appalls me?
>What hands are here? Ha! They pluck out mine eyes!
>Will all great Neptune's ocean wash these spots⁷
>Clean from this dress? No; this the dress will rather
>The multitudinous seas incarnadine,
>Making the green one white.

(Lady MacClinton returns.)

Lady MacClinton: My hands are of your color; but I shame
>To wear a heart so white.

(Knocking.)

>I hear a knocking
>At the south entry. Retire we to our chamber.

Act Two - Scene Three

A little water clears us of this deed.
How easy it is then! Your constancy
Hath left you unattended.

(Knocking.)

Hark! More knocking.
Get on your robe, lest occasion call us
And show us to be watchers; be not lost
So poorly in your thoughts.

MACCLINTON: To know my deed, 'twere best not know myself.

(Knocking.)

Wake Livingston with thy knocking! I would thou couldst!

(Exit both.)

SCENE FOUR

(Setting: a meeting room in the White House. Knocking within. Enter White House manservant.)

WHITE HOUSE MANSERVANT: Here's a knocking indeed! If a man were porter of hell gate, he would have grown old turning the key.

(Knocking.)

Knock, knock, knock! Who's there, in the name of Beelzebub? Here is a farmer, who farmed on the expectation of plenty, and got hanged by Al Gore's environmental laws[1] and Kyoto Protocol.[2]

(Knocking.)

Knock, knock! Who's there, in the other devil's name? Faith, here's an equivocator, a damn Los Alamos Justice Department security lackey,[3] who could swear in both the scales against either scale, who committed treason enough for China's sake, yet could not equivocate to heaven. O, come in equivocator.

(Knocking.)

Knock, knock, knock! Who's there? Faith, here's a Red Chinese Army businessman[4] come hither, for stealing out of a Buddhist monks' Democratic fundraiser.[5] Come in, Red Chinaman,[6] here you may roast your goose.

(Knocking.)

Knock, knock! Never at quiet! What are you? But this place is too cold for hell. I'll devil-porter it no further. I had thought to have let in some of all professions, that go the primrose way to the everlasting bonfire.

(Knocking.)

Anon, anon! I pray you, remember the White House interns. *(Opens the door.)*

(Enter Harry and Tom.)

HARRY: Was it so late, Friend, ere you went to bed,
That you do lie so late?
WHITE HOUSE MANSERVANT: Faith, sir, we were carousing 'til the second cock, and drink, sir, is a great provoker of three things.

Act Two - Scene Four

HARRY: What three things does drink especially provoke?

WHITE HOUSE MANSERVANT: Sir, nose-painting, sleep, and urine. Lechery, Sir, it provokes and unprovokes. It provokes the desire, but it takes away the performance. Therefore, much drink may be said to be an equivocator with lechery. It makes him, and it mars him; it sets him on, and it takes him off; it persuades him, and disheartens him; makes him stand to, and not stand to. In conclusion, equivocates him in a sleep, and giving him the lie, leaves him.

HARRY: I believe drink gave thee the lie last night.

WHITE HOUSE MANSERVANT: That it did, Sir, in the very throat on me. But I requited him for his lie; and, I think, being too strong for him, though he took up my legs sometimes, yet I made a shift to cast him.

HARRY: Is thy master stirring?

(*Enter* MACCLINTON.)

Our knocking has awakened him; here he comes.

TOM: Good-morrow, noble sir.

MACCLINTON: Good-morrow, both.

HARRY: Is the queen stirring, worthy thane?

MACCLINTON: Not yet.

HARRY: She did command me to call timely on her;
    I have almost slipped the hour.

MACCLINTON: I'll bring you to her.

HARRY: I know this is a joyful trouble to you;
    But yet 'tis one.

MacClinton

MacClinton: The labor we delight in physics pain.
   This is the door.
Harry: I'll make so bold to call,
   For 'tis my limited service. (*Exits.*)
Tom: Goes the queen hence today?
MacClinton: She does. She did appoint so.
Tom: The night has been unruly. Where we lay,
   Our chimneys were blown down, and, as they say,
   Lamentings heard in the air, strange screams of death,
   And prophesying with accents terrible
   Of dire combustion and confused events
   New hatched to the woeful time. The obscure bird
   Clamored the livelong night; some say, the Earth
   Was feverous and did shake.
MacClinton: 'Twas a rough night.
Tom: My young remembrance cannot parallel
   A fellow to it.

(*Enter Harry with a horrified look on his face.*)

Harry: O horror! Horror! Horror! Tongue, nor heart,
   Cannot conceive nor name thee!
MacClinton: Harry, what's the matter?
Harry: Confusion now hath made his masterpiece!
   Most sacrilegious murder hath broke ope
   The lord's anointed temple, and stole thence
   The life of the building.
MacClinton: What is it you say? The life?
Tom: Mean you her majesty, the Queen?

Act Two - Scene Four

HARRY: Approach the chamber, and destroy your sight
> With a new Gorgon. Do not bid me speak;
> See, and then speak yourselves.

TOM and HARRY (*fleeing in terror while screaming*): Awake! Awake!
> Ring the alarm bell! Murder and treason! Awake!
> Shake off this downy sleep, death's counterfeit,
> And look on death itself! Up, up, and see
> The great doom's image!
> As from your graves rise up, and walk like sprites
> To countenance this horror! Ring the bell.

(*Bell rings. Enter Lady MacClinton, her hair in rollers and night cream on her face.*)

LADY MACCLINTON: What's the business,
> That such a hideous trumpet calls to parley
> The sleepers of the house? Speak, speak!

MACCLINTON: O, gentle lady,
> 'Tis not for you to hear what I speak.
> The repetition, in a woman's ear,
> Would murder as fell.
> But, Honeybunch, you kinda need to fix yourself up a bit,
> Before you wander about the White House.
> You keep scaring the help with your night war paint and cold cream.

(*Curtain*)

ACT THREE

Scene One

(Setting: east banquet room of the White House. Dick is standing by the door. The music "Hail to the Chief" plays as MacClinton enters the room with Lady MacClinton, Tom, Harry, assorted White House aides and guests, and MacLivingston.[1])

DICK: Thou hast it now, Governor, then President, and now President again, all
    As the weird women promised, and I fear
    Thou play'dest most foully for it. Yet it was said
    It should not stand in thy posterity,
    But that thyself should be the root and father
    Of many kings. If there come truth from them—
    As upon thee, MacClinton, their speeches shine—
    Why, but by the verities on thee made good,
    May they not be my oracles as well,
    And set me in hope? But hush, no more.

MacClinton

MacClinton: Here's our chief guest.
Lady MacClinton: If he had been forgotten,
> It had been as a gap in our great feast,
> And all things unbecoming.

MacClinton: Tonight we hold a solemn supper, Sir,
> And I'll request your presence.

MacLivingston: Let your highness
> Command upon me, to the which my duties
> Are with a most indissoluble tie
> Forever knit.

MacClinton: Ride you this afternoon?
MacLivingston: Ay, my good lord.
MacClinton: We should have else desired your good advice
> Which still hath been both grave and prosperous
> In this day's Security Council; but we'll take tomorrow.
> Is it far you ride?

MacLivingston: As far, my lord, as will fill up the time
> 'Twixt this and supper. Go not my flight the better,
> I must become a borrower of the night
> For a dark hour or twain.

MacClinton: Fail not our feast.
MacLivingston: My lord, I will not.
MacClinton: We hear our bloody cousins are bestowed
> In the South and in the Midwest, not confessing
> Their cruel parricide, filling their hearers
> With strange invention. But of that tomorrow,
> When therewithal we shall have cause of state
> Craving us jointly. Hie you to horse, adieu,
> 'Til you return at night. Goes MacGingrich with you?

Act Three - Scene One

MACLIVINGSTON: Ay, my good lord, our time does call upon
  his.
MACCLINTON: I wish your flight swift and sure of foot.
  And so I do commend you to their backs.
  Farewell.
  (*Exit MacLivingston.*)
  Let every man be master of his time
  'Til seven at night; to make society
  The sweeter welcome, we will keep ourself
  'Til supper time alone. When then, God be with you!

(*All depart but MacClinton and White House Aide.*)

  Aide, a word with you. Attend those men
  Our pleasure?
WHITE HOUSE AIDE: They are, my lord, without the East Gate.[2]
MACCLINTON: Bring them before us.

(*Exit White House Aide.*)

  To be thus is nothing,
  But to be safely thus, our fears in Livingston
  Stick deep, and in his royalty of nature
  Reigns that which would be feared. 'Tis much he dares,
  And, to that dauntless temper of his mind,
  He hath a wisdom that doth guide his valor
  To act in safety. There is none but he
  Whose being I do fear; and under him
  My genius is rebuked, as it is said
  Mark Anthony's was by Caesar. He chided the sisters,

MacClinton

> When they first put the name of President upon me,
> And bade them speak to him; then prophet-like
> They hailed him father to a line of Republican Speakers of the House.
> Upon my head they placed a fruitless crown,
> And put a barren scepter in my grip,
> Thence to wrenched with an unlineal hand,
> No son of mine succeeding. If it be so,
> For Livingston's issue have I filled my mind,
> For them the gracious MacDole have I politically murdered,
> Put rancors in the vessel of my peace
> Only for them, and mine eternal jewel
> Given to the common enemy of man,
> To make them kings, the seed of Livingston kings!
> Rather than so, come Fate into the list,
> And champion me to the utterance. *(pauses)* Who's there?

(Enter White House Aide with two Character Assassins.)
> Now go to the door, and stay there 'til we call.

(Exit White House Aide.)
> Can't be too careful now with that Supreme Court ruling[3]
> That the Secret Service and White House staffers have to testify truthfully.
> Was it not yesterday we spoke together?

CHARACTER ASSASSIN 1: It was, so please your highness.

MACCLINTON: Well, then, now
> Have you considered my speeches? Know

Act Three - Scene One

That it was he, in times past, which held you
So under fortune, which you thought had been
Our innocent self. This I made good to you
In our last conference; He was the one that spoke
Against pornography and led the fight to limit its sale.[4]
I'm all for the free exchange of sex, although that Flowery article in *Penthouse*[5] was a little embarrassing;
He passed in probation with you,
How you were borne in hand, how crossed, the instruments,
Who wrought with them, and all things else that might
To half a soul and to a notion crazed
Say, "Thus did Livingston and those Republicans."

CHARACTER ASSASSIN 1: You made it known to us.

MACCLINTON: I did so; and went further, which is now
Our point of second meeting. Do you find
Your patience so predominant in your nature.
That you can let this go? Are you gospelled,
To pray for this good man, and for his issue,
Whose heavy hand hath bowed you to the grave
And beggared yours forever?

CHARACTER ASSASSIN 1: We are men, my liege.

MACCLINTON: You ought to hear Hillary go off on the subject of men.
On second thought, maybe you shouldn't. But anyway,
In the catalog you go for men,
As hounds and greyhounds, mongrels, spaniels, curs,
Sloughs, water rugs, and demiwolves, are clept
All by the name of dogs: the valued file

MacClinton

    Distinguishes the swift, the slow, the subtle,
    The housekeeper, the hunter, every one
    According to the gift which bounteous nature
    Hath in him closed, whereby he does receive
    Particular attention, from the bill
    That writes them all alike, and so of men.
    Now, if you have a station in the file,
    Not in the worst rank of manhood, say it,
    And I will put that business in your bosoms,
    Whose execution takes your enemy off,
    Grapples you to the heart and love of us
    Who wear our health but sickly in his life,
    Which in his death were perfect.

CHARACTER ASSASSIN 2: I am one, my liege.
    Whom the vile blows and buffets of the world
    Hath so incensed that I am reckless what
    I do to spite the world.

CHARACTER ASSASSIN 1: And I another
    So wear with disasters, tugged with fortune,
    That I would set my life on any chance,
    To mend it, or be rid of it.
    I have heard a penthouse[6] full of anger at those
    Who have made me a Hustler.[7]
    They who talk of morality
    And in their own lives have ever stumbled.
    They need to be destroyed.
    I'll give a million reasons to anyone[8]
    Who will help me get the dirt
    On such Republican politicians.

Act Three - Scene One

MacClinton: Both of you
    Know Livingston is your enemy.
Character Assassins 1 and 2: True, my lord.
MacClinton: So is he mine. And in such bloody distance,
    That every minute of his being thrusts
    Against my near'st of life. And though I could
    With barefaced lies and power sweep him from my sight,
    And bid my will avouch it, yet I must not,
    For certain friends that are both his and mine,
    Whose loves I may not drop, but wail his fall
    Who I myself struck down.
    Besides, there may be a limit to what Reno[9]
    And the IRS will do to destroy my enemies
    And cover up my sins. Thence it is
    That I to your assistance do make love,
    Masking the business from the common eye,
    For sundry weighty reasons.
Character Assassin 2: We shall, my lord,
    Perform what you command us.
Character Assassin 1: Though our lives . . .
MacClinton: Your spirits shine through you.
    Within this hour at most
    I will advise you where to plant yourselves,
    Acquaint you with the perfect spy of the time,
    The moment on it, for it must be done tonight,
    Because the impeach vote looms.[10]
    And something from the White House; always thought
    That I require a clearness. And with him

MacClinton

> Leave no rubs or botches in the work.
> And anyone else who keeps him company on that side of the aisle,
> Whose absence is no less material to me
> Than is his father's, must embrace the fate
> Of that dark hour. Resolve yourselves apart;
> I'll come to you anon.

CHARACTER ASSASSINS 1 AND 2: We are resolved, my lord.

MACCLINTON: I'll call upon you straight; abide within,
> Until the reporters outside leave, so you can leave unseen.

(Exit Character Assassins.)

SCENE TWO

(Setting: a room in the White House presidential quarters. Enter Lady MacClinton and servant.)

LADY MACCLINTON: Is Livingston gone from the White House?

SERVANT: Ay, Madam, but returns again tonight.

LADY MACCLINTON: Say to the President, I would attend his leisure
For a few words.

SERVANT: Madam, I will. *(Exits.)*

LADY MACCLINTON: If Monica isn't attending his leisure right now.
I swear, I bet she could take "the chrome off a trailer hitch."[1]
Nought is had, all is spent, especially Bill,
Where our desire is got without content.
'Tis safer to be that which we destroy
Than by destruction dwell in doubtful joy.

(Enter MacClinton.)

MacClinton

How now, my lord! Why do you keep alone,
Of sorriest fancies your companies making,
Using those thoughts which should indeed have died
With them they think on? Things without all remedy
Should be without regard. What's done, is done.

MACCLINTON: We have scotched the snake, not killed it. [2]
She'll close and be herself, whilst our poor malice
Remains in danger of her former tooth. [3]
But let the frame of things disjoint, both the worlds suffer,
Ere we will eat our meal in fear and sleep
In the affliction of these terrible dreams
That shake us nightly. Better be with the dead,
Whom we, to gain our peace, have sent to peace,
Than on the torture of the mind to lie
In restless ecstasy.

LADY MACCLINTON: Bill, I don't want to hear anything else about your girlfriends!

MACCLINTON: I'm not talking about girls, Hill. I'm talking about the Republicans!
MacDole's presidential hopes are in the grave;
After a long political life's fitful fever, his political future sleeps well;
Treason has done his worst; nor steel, nor poison,
Malice domestic, foreign levy, nothing,
Can touch him further.

LADY MACCLINTON: Come on;
Gentle my lord, sleep o'er your rugged looks,
Be bright and jovial among your guests tonight.

Act Three - Scene Two

MacClinton: So shall I, Love, and so I pray be you.
  Let your remembrance apply to Livingston;
  Present him eminence, both with eye and tongue.
  Unsafe the while, that we
  Must wash our honors in these flattering streams,
  And make our faces masks to our hearts,
  Disguising what they are.
Lady MacClinton: You must leave this.
MacClinton: O, full of scorpions is my mind, dear Wife!
  Thou knowest that Livingston lives and will be the next Speaker of the House.
  And Livingston is no MacGingrich.[4]
Lady MacClinton: But in those Republicans nature's copy is not eternal.
MacClinton: There's comfort yet; they are assailable,
  Then be thou jocund, in high spirits, ere the bat has flown
  His cloistered flight, ere to a black widow's summons
  The shard-borne beetle with his drowsy hums
  Hath rung night's yawning peal, there shall be done
  A deed of dreadful note.
Lady MacClinton: What's to be done?
MacClinton: Be innocent of the knowledge, dearest chick,
  'Til thou applaud the deed. Come, sealing night,
  Scarf up the tender eye of the pitiful day,
  And with thy bloody and invisible hand
  Cancel and tear to pieces that great bond
  Which keeps me paled! Light thickens, and the crow

MacClinton

>Makes wing to the rooky wood.
>Good things of day begin to droop and drowse,
>While night's black agents to their preys do rouse.
>Thou marvels at my words; behold thee 'til
>Things bad begun make strong themselves by ill.
>So, prithee, go with me.

(*Exit all.*)

Scene Three

(Setting: across the street from the Capitol building, near a cluster of trees. Enter both Character Assassins, Reporter, and Cameraman.)

Character Assassin 1: But who bid thee join with us?

Reporter: A news leak in the White House I have. Calls herself Deep Throat. Don't know who she is. I think it's an inside joke. I felt like MacClinton had her call. Those FBI files sure have been helpful though.

Character Assassin 2: He needs not our mistrust, since he delivers
Our offices and what we have to do,
To the direction just.

Character Assassin 1: Then stand with us.
The west yet glimmers with some streaks of day.
Now spurs the lated traveler apace
To gain the timely inn, and near approaches
The subject of our watch.

MacClinton

REPORTER: Hark! I hear a car approaching.

(MacLivingston and Aide get out of the car in front of the Capitol steps.)

MACLIVINGSTON: Give us a light there, ho!

CHARACTER ASSASSIN 2: Then 'tis he; the rest
    That are within the note of expectation
    Already are in the court.

REPORTER: 'Tis he.

CHARACTER ASSASSIN 1: Stand to it.

MACLIVINGSTON *(speaking to Aide)*: It will be rain tonight.

CHARACTER ASSASSIN 1: Let it come down.

(They cross the street to MacLivingston. The Cameraman's camera light catches him by surprise, making him look like a deer caught in the headlights.)

REPORTER: Representative MacLivingston, we have proof you had an affair within the past twenty years. Representative MacLivingston, how can you support morality and not be perfect?[1] Is it true? Do you deny it?

MACLIVINGSTON: O, treachery! Fly, good Aide, fly, fly, fly! Thou mayst revenge. What? When? Who? Who are ya'll?

REPORTER: So you are denying, are you? Did you get that on film?

CAMERAMAN: Yeah, got it all.

REPORTER: OK. Let's get this back to the station for the evening news broadcast. This will really get us some ratings. What a scoop!

Act Three - Scene Three

MacLivingston (*looking stunned*): But, who? What are ya'll talking about? I'll try to answer your questions. Wait!

Reporter: That's OK. We got everything we need in the can.
   (*to Character Assassin 1*): Thanks for the tips. You scratch our backs, and we'll scratch yours.

(*Exit all. Curtain.*)

ACT FOUR

SCENE ONE

(*Setting: mobile-home kitchen and living room area with green shag carpeting and black-velvet painting of Elvis Presley. Lots of tall, thick candles are burning. The walls and coffee table contain New Age symbols and objects like pentagrams and crystals, and a Ouija board is on the table. A large stew pot with lid is on the stove. Scattered on the kitchen counters and near the stove are saucers, bowls, spoons, and cookbooks.*

It is night. Through the uncurtained windows, the darkness is lit sporadically by flashes of lightning; and thunder claps occasionally. As the scene progresses, the thunder and lightning occur closer together until the moment MacClinton opens the door later.

Enter the three *itches.)

*ITCH 1: Three times last night my striped cat meowed and woke me up.

*ITCH 2: Well, three times last night, my daughter's hedgehog whined and woke me up.

MacClinton

*ITCH 3 *(taking the lid off the stew pot and stirring it with a ladle)*: It's time, it's time.

*ITCHES 1-3: Double, double, toil and trouble;
  Fire, burn, cauldron, bubble.

*ITCH 1 *(looking in the cookbook, running her finger along a recipe)*: Fillet of a fenny snake,
  In the cauldron boil and bake.

*ITCH 2: Sister, what are you cooking?

*ITCH 1: I caught the eye of Newt last night, during the fog,
  Went out drinking, and now I need the hair of the dog.

(She looks in a cabinet and takes out a bottle of cheap whisky, pours a stiff drink, and drinks it straight.)

*ITCH 2: He's got an adder's forked tongue,
  And he's married.[1] And he's not even young!

*ITCH 1: Yeah, he's a charm of powerful trouble,
  Like a hell-broth boil and bubble.

*ITCH 3 *(looking out the window)*: Speaking of powerful trouble,
  Here comes a shark with the gall of a goat,
  Here comes Monica, again to gloat.

*ITCH 2 *(stirring the pot again with the ladle)*: Double, double, toil and trouble;
  Here comes Monica all a-bubble;
  Fire burn and big pot bubble.

*ITCH 1 *(taking the ladle and stirring a little, then looking back at the recipe)*:
  Cool it with alligator's blood,
  Then the food is firm and good.
  Boy, I love cooking Cajun food.

Act Four - Scene One

(Enter Monica, wearing a tight, blue dress stretched over her full figure and a black beret.)

MONICA: O, well done! I commend your pains,
    And every one shall share in the gains,
    And get fatter, and fatter, and fat. *(pats a woman on her ample bottom)*
    (sings in a scornful manner): And now about the cauldron you sing,
    Like elves and fairies in a ring,
    You're enchanting with all that you put in,
    But I go and enchant Bill, when I put out.

*(She laughs, turns, sways out, and slams the door behind her. The three *itches watch her go, their faces cold with anger.)*

*ITCH 1: Bitch.

*ITCH 2: Fat bitch.

*ITCH 3: Fat, stupid bitch.

*ITCHES 1-3: Bitch.

*(*itch 1 returns to her cooking, looking at the recipe book, and adding seasonings. All three women go to the living room area and sit on the couch and chairs. They make small talk, looking at New Age magazines and smoking cigarettes. Car lights flash through the window as a car pulls up to the mobile home. The car stops, and the engine is killed. A car door slams.)*

*ITCH 2: By the pricking of my thumbs,
    Something wicked this way comes.
    Open, locks,
    Whoever knocks!

MacClinton

(There is a single knock, then MacClinton opens the door and comes in with a sly, lecherous grin on his face. Now there is a simultaneous burst of lightning and thunderous clap of thunder, indicating the eye of the storm has arrived.)

MacClinton: How now, you secret, midnight hags!
    What is it you do?

*Itches 1-3: A deed without a name,
    Country cooking's our game.

MacClinton: I order you, but that which you profess
    However you come to know it answer me.
    Though you untie the winds and let them fight
    Against the churches;[2] though the El Niño waves[3]
    Confound and swallow navigation up;
    Though bladed corn be lodged and trees blown down;
    Though houses topple on their owners' heads;
    Though the treasure
    Of nature's gardens tumble all together,
    Even until destruction sicken Al Gore,[4]
    Everyone answer me what I ask of you.

*Itch 1: Speak.

*Itch 2: Demand.

*Itch 3: We'll answer.

*Itches 1-3: Just don't let MacStarr get a subpoena!

*Itch 1: Say if thou hadst rather hear it from our mouths,
    Or from our masters.

MacClinton: Call 'em, let me see 'em.

*Itch 1: We'll call 'em as we see 'em.

*Itches 1-3: Come, high or low,
    Thyself and office deftly show.

Act Four - Scene One

*(Thunder claps. Lights flicker. *itch 1 goes into a trance.)*

MACCLINTON: Tell me, thou unknown power.

*ITCH 2: He knows thy thought.
Hear his speech, but say thou naught.

*ITCH 1 *(in strange, low, guttural voice):*
MacClinton! MacClinton! MacClinton! Beware MacStarr.
Beware the special prosecutor. Dismiss me. Enough.

MACCLINTON: Whate'er thou art, for thy good caution, thanks;
Thou hast sharpened my fear aright. But one word more…

*ITCH 1: He will not be commanded; here's another,
More potent than the first.

*(A clap of thunder. The lights flicker again. *itch 2 goes into a trance.)*

*ITCH 2 *(in strange, quivering voice):* MacClinton! MacClinton! MacClinton!

MACCLINTON: Had I three ears, I'd hear thee.

*ITCH 2: Be bloody, bold, and resolute; laugh to scorn
The power of man. For no man of woman born
Shall harm MacClinton.

MACCLINTON: Then live, MacStarr; what need I fear of thee?
But yet I'll make assurance double sure,
And take a bond of fate. Thou shalt not live,
That I may tell my pale-hearted fear that it lies,
And then I can sleep in spite of thunder.

MacClinton

(A clap of thunder. The lights flicker. *itch 3 goes into a trance, stands, puts a large hoop on her head, and holds a small bonsai tree that was on the coffee table.)

MACCLINTON: What is this,
> That rises like the issue of a king,
> And wears upon her baby-brow the crown of sovereignty?

*ITCHES 1-3: Listen, but speak not to it.

*ITCH 3 *(speaking in high-pitched voice):* Be lion-mettled, proud, and take no care
> Who chafes, who frets, or where conspirators are.
> MacClinton shall never vanquished be until
> The Great Forest's tall, lean wood to the White House hill
> Shall come against him.

MACCLINTON: That will never be.
> Who can impress the forest, bid the tree
> To unfix his earthbound root? Good omens! Good.
> Rebellious dead, rise never, 'til the wood
> Of the Great Forest rise, and our high-placed MacClinton
> Shall leave the lease of nature, pay his breath
> To time and mortal custom. Yet my heart
> Throbs to know one thing; tell me, if your art
> Can tell so much: Shall Bush's issue[5] ever
> Reign in this kingdom again?

*ITCHES 1-3: *(in their regular voices):* Seek to know no more.

MACCLINTON: I will be satisfied. Deny me this,

Act Four - Scene One

And an eternal curse fall on you! Let me know.
(pauses) What noise is this?

*ITCH 1: Show!

*ITCH 2: Show!

*ITCH 3: Show!

*ITCHES 1-3: Show his eyes, and grieve his heart;
Come like shadows, so depart.

*(*itch 1 holds up a huge posterboard with photographs of the Bushes in a family gathering. Surrounding the family photo are large pictures of individual family members, each with a gold crown drawn on his or her head.)*

MACCLINTON: They art all too like the spirit of Bush. Down!
Thy crown does sear mine eyeballs. And thy hair,
Thou other gold-bound brow, is like the first President Bush.[6]
Is that George W.?[7] Isn't that Jeb?[8]
A third is like the former. Filthy hags!
Why do you show me this? A fourth.[9] Start, eyes!
What, will the line stretch out to the crack of doom?
Another yet? A seventh? I'll see no more.
And yet the eighth appears, who bears a glass
Which shows me many more; and some I see
That twofold balls and treble scepters carry.
Horrible sight! Now I see 'tis true,
For the defeated Bush smiles upon me,
And points at them for his. What, is this so?

*ITCH 1: Ay, sir, all this is so. But why
Stands MacClinton thus amazedly?

MacClinton

> Come, Sisters, cheer we up his spirits,
> And show the best of our delights.
> I'll charm the air to give a sound,
> While you perform your antic round.
> That this great king may kindly say
> Our duties did his welcome pay.

*(Music. The *itches dance, and vanish out the door.)*

MacClinton: Where are they? Gone? Let this pernicious hour
> Stand accursed in the calendar.
> Come in, without there!

(Enter Driver.)

Driver: What's your grace's will?

MacClinton: Saw you the weird sisters?

Driver: No, my lord.

MacClinton: Came they not by you?

Driver: No, indeed, my lord.

MacClinton: Infected be the air whereon they ride,
> And damned all those that trust them! I did hear
> The galloping horsepower. Who was it came by?

Driver: 'Tis two or three, my lord, that bring you word
> MacStarr has fled to Arkansans.[10]

MacClinton: Fled to Arkansas?

Driver: Ay, my good lord.

MacClinton: Time, thou anticipates my dread exploits.
> The flighty purpose never is o'ertook

Act Four - Scene One

Unless the deed go with it. From this moment
The firstlings of my heart shall be
The firstlings of my hand. And even now
To crown my thoughts with acts, be it thought and done.
The home of MacStarr I will surprise,
Seize upon his latest report, and give it the edge of the sword
Of my sanctimonious attack on my next weekly radio broadcast.
I'll attack his wife, his babes, and all unfortunate souls
That trace him in his line. No boasting like a fool.
But no more sights! Where are these gentlemen?
Come, bring me where they are.

(Exit all.)

SCENE TWO

(Setting: MacStarr's home. Enter Lady MacStarr, her son, and a lawyer from the office of the special prosecutor.)

LADY MACSTARR: What has he done, to make him fly the land?

LAWYER: You must have patience, Lady MacStarr.

LADY MACSTARR: He has none.
>His flights are madness; even when our actions are logical,
>Our fears make us scared.

LAWYER: You know not
>Whether it was his wisdom or his fear.
>That caused him to take this job.

LADY MACSTARR: Wisdom! To leave his wife, to leave his babes,[1]
>His mansion and his titles, the law firm, and instead
>From whence he does fly?
>Even the poor wren,
>The most diminutive of birds, will fight for

MacClinton

      Her young ones in her nest, against the owl.
      And so provide for its own.
      And little is the wisdom, where the flight
      Back and forth across the country,
      So runs against all reason,
      Even though for the noblest duty
      As Special Prosecutor.
LAWYER: My dearest cousin,
      Calm yourself. But, for your husband,
      He is noble, wise, judicious, and best knows
      The fits of the season. I dare not speak much further,
      But these are cruel times, when we are called traitors
      And do not know ourselves; when we hear rumor
      About what we fear, yet know not what we fear,
      But float upon a wild and violent sea,
      Each way and more. I take my leave of you.
      I shall not be long, but I'll be here again soon.
      Things at the worst will either cease, or else climb upward
      To what they were before. My pretty cousin,
      Blessings upon you!

Scene Three

(Setting: manicured front lawn of a beautiful Arlington, Virginia, home. Enter Lady MacWilley[1] and her son, who stroll the lawn.)

Lady MacWilley *(musing to herself)*: Fathered he is, and yet he's fatherless.[2]
    I am so much a fool, should I stay longer
    It would be my disgrace and my discomfort.
    I need to take my leave at once.
    And get out of this quagmire at once.
    (to child): Your father is dead,
    And what will you do now? How will you live?
Son: As birds do, Mother.
Lady MacWilley: What, with worms and flies?
Son: With what I get, I mean, and so do they.
Lady MacWilley: Poor bird! Would that you never have to fear the nets or traps or

MacClinton

    The pitfalls of the MacClinton smear machine.[3]
    It is a vast left-wing conspiracy![4]
    He snares us in, then does abuse and destroys us.
    Poor, dumb birds that know nothing,
    Or that cannot tell the reporters anything.
SON: Why should I fear, mother?
    It's the poor birds those traps are set for, right?
    My father is not dead, for all your saying.
LADY MACWILLEY: Yes, he is dead.
    Remember, on the day he died was when I went to see
    MacClinton to try to get a job to support us.
    It was in the Oval Office hallway he did assault me.
    Remember, I told you that.
SON: Oh, yeah, now I remember you telling me that, Mother.
LADY MACWILLEY: How will you do for a father?
SON: Nay, how will you do for a husband?
    You know MacClinton. From what I've seen on the
        news, if his wife has any honor,[5]
    Surely she has kicked him out. He may be available now.
LADY MACWILLEY: Why, I can buy me twenty at any market,
    At least as good as MacClinton.
SON: Then you'll buy 'em to sell again.
LADY MACWILLEY: But who would take *him* off my hands?
    Thou speakest with all thy wit, and yet faith
    With wit enough for thee.
SON: Is MacClinton a traitor, Mother?
LADY MACWILLEY: Ay, that he is.
SON: What is a traitor?
LADY MACWILLEY: Why, one who swears and lies.

Act Four - Scene Three

Son: And be all traitors that do so?

Lady MacWilley: Every one who does so is a traitor and must be hanged.

Son: And must they all be hanged that swear and lie?

Lady MacWilley: Every one.

Son: Who must hang them?

Lady MacWilley: Why, the honest men.

Son: Then the liars and swearers are fools; for there are liars and swearers enough in Washington to beat the honest men and hang them up.

Lady MacWilley: Especially in the Senate.[6] Now God help thee, poor monkey! But how wilt thou do for a father?

(Enter Jogger who comes up to MacWilley and son in yard.)

Jogger: Bless you, fair dame! I am not known to you,
  Though of your state of honor I am perfectly aware.
  I believe some danger does approach you soon.
  If you will take a homely man's advice,
  Be not found here when they come to serve the subpoena;[7]
  Run hence, with your little one. *(Pats the child's head.)*

(Lady MacWilley, terrified, pulls son to her to protect him.)

  To scare you thus, I think I am too savage;
  But I'd feel worse if you were felled with cruelty,
  Which is too nigh your person. Heaven preserve you!
  I abide no longer. Run. Save yourself.
  (in a menacing voice): But you are warned:

MacClinton

>Speak to no one about MacClinton, especially to MacStarr.
>You have been warned. And we know where you live. *(Pats the child's head.)*
>And we know who you love. You've been warned. *(Turns and jogs away.)*

LADY MACWILLEY: Whither should I fly?
>I have done no harm. But I remember now.
>I am in this earthly world; here in Washington, to do harm
>Is often laudable, to do good sometime
>Accounted dangerous folly. Why then, alas,
>Do I put up that womanly defense,
>To say I have done no harm?
>I did nothing. I just went to look for a job,
>And he attacked me. It is the truth.
>But where is the media to defend the truth?[8]
>They worship at his feet, receiving his crumbs,
>And leaving us his regurgitated words and their crap.

(Curtain)

ACT FIVE

Scene One

(*Setting: a room in the White House presidential quarters. Enter Doctor and Aide to the First Lady.*)

DOCTOR: I have two nights watched with you, but can perceive no truth in your report. When was it she last walked?

AIDE: Since her husband went into the campaign field last week, I have seen her rise from her bed, throw her nightgown on her, unlock her closet, take forth a box labeled "Whitewater papers,"[1] take out a paper, fold it, write on it, read it, seal it, and again return to bed—yet all this while in a most fast sleep.

DOCTOR: It is a great perturbation in nature to receive at once the benefit of sleep and do the effects of watching! In this slumbery agitation, besides her walking and other actual actions, what, at any time, have you heard her say?

AIDE: That, sir, I will not report about her.

DOCTOR: You may to me, and it is most necessary you should.

MacClinton

AIDE: Neither to you nor any one, I having no witness to confirm my speech. Had I but tape recorded her words, lest I later be tripped[2] by MacClinton's defenders.

(Enter Lady MacClinton with a blue dress in her hands.)

AIDE: Look, here she comes! This is how she acts, and upon my life, she's fast asleep. Observe her, stand close.

DOCTOR: How came she by that dress?[3]

AIDE: Why, it hung by her bed. She has the dress by her continually; it is her command.

DOCTOR: You see, her eyes are open.

AIDE: Ay, but their sense is shut.

DOCTOR: What is it she does now? Look, how she rubs the dress with her hands.

AIDE: It is an accustomed action with her, to seem thus washing it with her hands. I have known her to continue in this a quarter of an hour.

LADY MACCLINTON: Yet here's a spot.

DOCTOR: Listen, she speaks! I will write down what she says, to satisfy my memoirs more strongly.

LADY MACCLINTON: Out, damned spot![4] Out, I say! One, two; why, then 'tis time to do it. Hell is murky! Fie, my lord, fie! A soldier and afeard?
  What need we fear who knows it, when none can call our power to accomplish it?
  Yet who would have thought my old man to have had so much in him?
  Out, damned spot! Out, I say!

DOCTOR: Did you catch that?

Act Five - Scene One

LADY MACCLINTON: The President has a wife; what about her now? What, will this dress ne'er be clean? No more of that, my Bill, no more of that. You mar all with that starting, with all this going and coming. And, Bill, you promised to never stray again. *(Continues to rub the spots on the dress, tears running down her face.)*

DOCTOR: Go, go; we know what we should not.

AIDE: She has spoken what she should not, I am sure of that; heaven knows what she has known.

LADY MACCLINTON: Everywhere there's the smell of
That woman, Miss Lewinsky.

All the perfumes of Arabia will not sweeten this little hand. Always cleaning up after Bill, always cleaning up his messes.[5] And he promised. Never again. Oh! Oh! Oh!

DOCTOR: What a sigh is there! The heart is sorely charged.

AIDE: I would not have such a heart in my bosom, for all her money and power.

DOCTOR: Well, well, well.

AIDE: Pray God it be, Sir.

DOCTOR: This disease is beyond my practice; yet I have known those who have walked in their sleep who have died holily in their beds.

LADY MACCLINTON: Wash the dress, put on your party dress, look not so pale, put on a happy face. I'm not some stand-by-your-man woman, staying home baking cookies.[6] I chose to have a career. I tell you yet again, Foster's buried; he cannot come out of his grave.

DOCTOR: Even so?

LADY MACCLINTON: To bed, to bed; there's knocking at the gate.

MacClinton

> Come, come, come, come, give me your hand, Bill. What's done, cannot be undone. Come to bed with me, Bill, to bed, to bed, to bed.

(Exit Lady MacClinton, crying and still rubbing spots off the dress.)

DOCTOR: Will she go now to bed?

AIDE: Directly.

DOCTOR: Foul whisperings are abroad; unnatural deeds
    Do breed unnatural troubles. Infected minds
    To their deaf pillows will discharge their secrets.
    More needs she the divine than the physician.
    God, God forgive us all! Look after her,
    Remove from her all the means of all annoyance,
    And still keep your eyes upon her. So, good-night.
    Her condition has amazed me, and amazed my sight.
    I know what I think, but I dare not speak.

AIDE: Good-night, good doctor.

Scene Two

(Setting: patio at Camp David. Enter Tom, Dick, Harry, and MacFile. They pull chairs closely together and sit.)

Dick: The Elephant[1] power is near, led on by MacDeLay,[2]
    And his friend MacArmey[3] and the good MacStarr.
    Revenges burn in them; for their dear causes
    They would cause enough bleeding and the grim alarm
    To excite a dead man.

Harry: Near the South Lawn wood
    Shall we meet them, and that way are they coming.

Tom: Who knows if William Bennett[4] will be there with his brother?

MacFile: For certain, sir, he is not.
    I still have copies of the FBI files on all those Republicans.[5]

Harry: There is many unrough youths, that even now
    Protest their first of manhood.

MacClinton

> Those earnest young Republicans surely have recruited well!

DICK: What does the tyrant?

TOM: Hillary or Billary?

DICK: The great White House he strongly fortifies.
> Some say he's crazy; others that lesser hate him and are still loyal to him,
> Not many of those left though,
> Do call it valiant fury; but, for certain,
> He cannot buckle his respected cause
> Within the belt of the rule of law,
> Because the Supreme Court ruled against us again.
> What's that? Five losses, no victories?
> Of course, not only can he not buckle his cause,
> He can't even keep his pants buckled.

TOM: Now does he feel
> His secret trysts sticking to his hands;
> Now minute revolts constantly upbraid his breach of faith;
> Those he commands move only in command,
> Nothing in love: now does he feel his title
> Hang loose about him, like a giant's robe
> Upon a dwarfish thief.

DICK: Who can blame them?
> His pestered senses to recoil and start,
> When all that is within him does condemn
> Him for what he's done to his presidency?

HARRY: Well, we march on,
> To give obedience where 'tis truly owed.

Act Five - Scene Two

>We go to meet the med'cine of our sickly country's needs
>And with him, we'll the last of our energy purge our country's ills.

(turns to face passing White House aide)

>I heard you've got a book deal[6] and a TV commentator contract.[7]
>Good going. I'm glad somebody beside Billary and Hillary
>Got something besides a subpoena out of this sewer of an existence.

(Exit all.)

Scene Three

(Setting: Oval Room of the White House. Enter MacClinton, Doctor, and White House Aide.)

MacClinton: Bring me no more reports, let them all fly
  'Til the forest wood comes to the White House.
  I don't have any fear. What's the boy MacStarr?
  Was he not born of woman? Those spirits that seem to know
  All our mortal future have pronounced me thus:
  "Fear not, MacClinton, no man that's born of woman
  Shall e'er have power upon thee." Then fly, you false allies.
  Hillary was right, you never believed in us.
  Go and mingle with the Republicans.
  My mind and my heart
  Shall never sag with doubt nor shake with fear.

MacClinton

> (*turns to White House Aide*) The devil damn you, you cream-faced loon!
> Where did you get that goose look?

WHITE HOUSE AIDE: There are ten . . .

MACCLINTON: Geese, villain?

WHITE HOUSE AIDE: Subpoenas, Sir.

MACCLINTON: Go prick thy face and over-red thy fear,
> Thou lily-livered boy. What subpoenas?
> Death of thy soul! Those linen cheeks of thine
> Are counselors to fear. What subpoenas, whey-face?

WHITE HOUSE AIDE: The Senate's subpoenas, so please you.

MACCLINTON: Take thy face hence. Get outta here!

(*Exit Aide.*)

MACCLINTON (*shouting*): Butler! (*normal voice*) I am sick at heart
> When I behold—(*shouting*) Butler, I say!—(*normal voice*) this push
> Will cheer me up, or unseat me now.
> I have lived long enough. My way of life
> Is falling into retirement and old age,
> And that which should accompany old age,
> Like honor, love, obedience, troops of friends,
> I guess I can't look to have; but, in their stead,
> Curses, not out loud, but deep, I get mealy mouthed honor,
> Nice words to my face, and curses to my back.
> (*shouting*) Butler!

(*Enter Butler.*)

Act Five - Scene Three

BUTLER: What is your gracious pleasure?

MACCLINTON: What is the latest news?

BUTLER: All is confirmed, Mr. President, which was reported on CNN this morning.

MACCLINTON: I'll fight, 'til from my bones my flesh be hacked.
    Give me my power tie[1] that Monica gave, uh, that I have there.

BUTLER: 'Tis not needed yet.
    The subpoena says you don't have to testify until next week.

MACCLINTON: I'll put it on.
    Send out more press spokesmen, scour the country round,
    Hang those that talk of fear. Give me my tie.
    How goes your patient, Doctor?

DOCTOR: She's not so sick, Mr. President,
    As she is troubled with nightmares,
    That keep her from rest.

MACCLINTON: Cure her of that.
    Canst thou not minister to a sick mind,
    Pluck from the memory a rooted sorrow,
    Raze out the troubles written in the brain,
    And with some sweet antidote obliviate
    And cleanse her troubled heart of that perilous stuff
    Which weighs upon her heart?

DOCTOR: Therein the patient
    Must minister to herself,
    Or else *(looking hard at MacClinton)* cut off that which causes her pain.

MacClinton

MacClinton: Throw this doctor to the dogs,
   Let Buddy² have him, I'll have none of it.
   Come, put my tie and jacket on; call me my staff;
   Butler, send out; Doctor, fly from me;
   Come on, hurry. If thou could, Doctor, cast about,
   Find her disease,
   And purge it to a sound and pristine health,
   I would applaud you at the very end
   Of my next State of the Union address,
   That should applaud again. Pull it off, I say.
   Isn't there some wonder drug that will
   Get rid of these Republicans? Hear'st thou of them?
   A couple of them take Viagra³ and now they all think they are young pups,
   Hot on my scent. Haven't you heard them?
Doctor: Ay, my good lord; your royal preparation
   Makes us hear something.
MacClinton: Bring it after me.
   I will not be afraid of death and destruction
   'Til the forest wood comes to the White House.

(*Exit MacClinton and Butler.*)

Scene Four

(Setting: park across the street from the front Capitol Hill steps. Enter MacHyde,[1] MacGingrich,[2] MacDeLay, and several House judiciary staffers.)

MacHyde: Friends, I hope, the days are near at hand
    That our House and Senate chambers will be safe.

MacGingrich: We don't doubt it.

Judiciary Staffer: What place is this before us?

MacGingrich: The Tidal Basin,[3] and over there is the White House.

MacHyde: Let everybody hew him down a bough of this
    Cherry limb sprig, with its spring flowers,[4]
    And bear it before him to his wife for putting up with
        these long hours this year.
    Is everyone ready to head up to the White House?
    Let us shadow the impeachment numbers from our
        host,

MacClinton

> And make his discovery of our numbers
> Err in his report of us.

JUDICIARY STAFFER: It shall be done.

MACDELAY: We've learned that the confident tyrant
> Keeps still in the White House, and will endure
> Our setting down before it.

MACHYDE: 'Tis his main hope,
> For where there is advantage to be given,
> Both more and less have given him their resignations,
> From soccer moms to all women, his support has waned,
> And none serve with him but those constrained by huge retainers,
> And whose hearts are absent too.

MACDELAY: Let our just censures,[5] after the impeachment vote,
> Attend the true event, and let's put on
> Industrious statesmanship.

MACHYDE: The time approaches,
> That will with due decision make us know
> What we need to say, we have said, and what we owe, we'll pay later.
> Thoughts are speculative, our hopes unsure, about success.
> But certain issues we must arbitrate,
> Which advance the war on MacClinton.

Scene Five

(Setting: White House balcony overlooking the West Lawn garden. Enter MacClinton and Dick.)

MacClinton: Hang out our banners on the outward walls;
    The cry is still, "They come." Our home is our castle,
    And our strength is our lawyers' briefs, and through them,
    We will laugh a siege to scorn. Here let them lie in the Tidal Basin
    'Til famine and the next election eat them up.
    Were they not forced with those that should be ours,
    We might have met them dareful, beard to beard,
    And beat them backward home.

(A cry and the shriek of women from inside.)

    What is that noise?

MacClinton

DICK: It is the cry of women, my good lord. *(Exits.)*
MACCLINTON: I have almost forgot the taste of fears.
    The time has been, my senses would have cooled
    To hear a night-shriek, and my hair
    Would at a dismal treatise rouse and stir and stand on end
    As life were in it. I have supped full with horrors;
    Direness, familiar to my slaughterous thoughts,
    Cannot once startle me.

(Dick reenters.)

    Wherefore was that cry?
DICK: The queen, my lord, is deadly,
    She's chasing Monica through the living quarters.
    She caught Monica trying to sneak to the Oval Office to see you.
MACCLINTON: She should have tried hereafter;
    There would have been a time for such a word.
    Tomorrow, and tomorrow, and tomorrow,
    Creeps in this petty pace from day to day,
    To the last syllable of recorded time;
    And all our yesterdays have lighted fools
    The way to dusty death. Out, out, brief candle!
    Life's but a walking shadow, a poor player
    That struts and frets his hour upon the stage,
    And then is heard no more.[1] It is a tale
    Told by an idiot, full of sound and fury,
    Signifying nothing.

(Enter Messenger.)

Act Five - Scene Five

    Thou com'st to use thy tongue, thy story quickly.
MESSENGER: Gracious my lord,
    I should report that which I say I saw,
    But know not how to do it.
MACCLINTON: Well, say, Sir.
MESSENGER: As I did stand my watch upon the hill,
    I looked toward the Capitol, and anon, methought
    The wood began to move.
MACCLINTON: Liar and slave!
MESSENGER: Let me endure your wrath, if it be not so;
    Within this three mile may you see it coming.
    I say, a moving grove.
MACCLINTON: If thou speakest false,
    Upon the next tree shalt thou hang alive,
    'Til famine cling thee; if thy speech be sooth,
    I care not if thou dost for me as much.
    I pull in resolution, and begin
    To doubt the equivocation of the fiend
    That lies like truth. "Fear not, 'til the forest wood
    Do comes to the White House;" and now a wood
    Comes toward the White House. Arm, arm, and out!
    If this which he avouches does appear,
    There is not flying hence nor tarrying here.
    I begin to be aweary of the sun,
    And wish the estate of the world were now undone.
    Ring the alarm bell! Blow, wind! Come, wrack!
    At least we'll die with harness on our back.

Scene Six

(Setting: White House before the East Gate with the flag flying. Several marching drummers are playing. Enter MacStarr, MacHyde, MacGingrich, and their support staff, all with small twigs pinned to their lapels.)

MacHyde: Now near enough, your leafy screens throw down,
    And show like those you are. You, worthy uncle,
    Shall with my cousin your right-noble son
    Lead our first battle. Worthy MacStarr and we
    Shall take upon what else remains to do,
    According to our order.

MacGingrich: Fare you well.
    Do we but find the tyrant's power tonight,
    Let us be beaten, if we cannot fight.

MacStarr: Make all our trumpets speak; give them all breath,
    Those clamorous harbingers of blood and death.

Scene Seven

(Setting: MacClinton is standing on another part of the White House lawn.)

MacClinton: They have tied me to a stake; I cannot fly,
> But bear-like I must fight the course.[1] What's he
> Who was not born of woman? Such a one
> Am I to fear, or none.

(Enter Young Republican.)

Young Republican: What is thy name?
MacClinton: Thou shalt be afraid to hear it.
Young Republican: No; though thou callest thyself a hotter name
> Than any is in hell.
MacClinton: My name's MacClinton.
Young Republican: That's the one!

MacClinton

> The devil himself could not pronounce a title
> More hateful to mine ear.

MACCLINTON: No, nor more fearful.

YOUNG REPUBLICAN: Thou liest, abhorred tyrant. I'll prove the lie thou speakest.

MACCLINTON: Thou wast born of woman.
> But swords I smile at, weapons laugh to scorn,
> Brandished by man that is of a woman born.

(Young Republican turns and runs. Alarms sound. Enter MacStarr.)

MACSTARR: That way the noise is. Tyrant, show thy face!
> If thou be defeated and with no stroke of mine,
> My wife and children's terrorized ghosts will haunt me still.
> I cannot strike at wretched kerns, whose arms
> Are hired to bear their staves; either thou, MacClinton,
> Or else the sharp cutting edge of my trial briefs with an unbattered edge
> I sheathe again unfiled. There thou shouldst be;
> By this great clatter before me, one of greatest note
> Seems to be located. Let me find him, fortune!

(Enter MacHyde and MacGingrich.)

MACGINGRICH: This way, my lord; the castle is gently rendered.
> The tyrant's people on both sides do fight,
> Half time in his defense, and half time as unnamed news sources.

Act Five - Scene Seven

> The noble thanes do bravely in the war,
> The day almost itself professes yours,
> And little is to do.

MACHYDE: We have met with foes
> That strike beside us.

MACGINGRICH: Enter, sir, the White House.

(Exit MacGingrich and MacHyde.)

MACCLINTON: Why should I play the Republican fool, and die
> On mine own sword, like Nixon's resignation?[2]
> While I see life, the gashes,
> Do better upon them.

MACSTARR: Turn, hell-hound, turn.

MACCLINTON *(surprise and hurt in his voice, with a tear in his eye[3])*: Me?
> Of all men else I have avoided thee.
> But get thee back, my soul is too much charged
> With blood of thine already.

MACSTARR: I have no words.
> My voice is in my special prosecutor designation,
> Thou bloodier villain
> Than prison terms can give thee out!

(MacStarr and MacClinton wrestle and shove each other.)

MACCLINTON *(with a smirk and sneer in his voice)*:
> You're wasting your breath. Thou losest labor.
> As easy mayst thou the entrenchment air
> With all thy keen sword impress

MacClinton

    As make me bleed crocodile tears for my misstatements,
    Let fall thy blade on vulnerable crests,
    Let your attacks fall on vulnerable heads,
    I live a charmed life, which must not yield,
    And I won't be undone by a man
    To a woman born.

MacStarr: Lose that charm,
    That voodoo you do so well won't work on me.
    And let the devil whom thou still hast served
    Tell thee, I may be a man of a woman born,
    But let me tell you, Monica is not a man
    To have been from her mother's womb
    Untimely ripped. She is a *woman!*
    And she has been talking to the special prosecutor's office about you,
    And about a certain bespotted blue dress,
    And about the Arkansas use of cigars, and about presents, and about meetings and about thong underwear,
    And about you having sex with that woman, Miss Lewinsky.[4]

MacClinton: Accursed be the tongue that tells me so,
    For it hath cowed my better part of man!
    And be these juggling fiends no more believed,
    That talk with us in a double sense,
    And toy with us, and then to speak to me in MacClinton doublespeak,
    That keep the word of promise to our ear,
    And break it to our hope.

Act Five - Scene Seven

MACSTARR: You're a fine one to speak against double-talk and half-truths.

MACCLINTON: I'll not fight thee.

MACSTARR: Then yield, you coward,
    And live to be the show and people will gaze on thee at times.
    We'll have thee caged, as our rarer monsters are,
    Painted upon a pole, and underwrit,
    Here may you see the tyrant.

MACCLINTON: I will not yield,
    Of course, when I said I'll not fight thee,
    My meaning depended on what the word *I'll* meant,[5]
    And what the word *not* meant,
    And what the word *fight* meant,
    And what the word *thee* meant.
    I'll not kiss the ground before your feet,
    And to be baited with the Republican rabble's curse,
    Though the wooden Gore[6] be come to the White House,
    And thou opposed, together with that woman, Miss Lewinsky,
    Who is not a man of a woman born,
    Yet I will try the last. Before my body
    I throw my warlike shield; lay on MacStarr,
    And damned be him that first cries, "Hold, enough."

(They lunge for each other's throats, wrestling together.)

MACCLINTON: Damn you, you Republican piss-ant.

MACSTARR: Damn you, you Democratic perjurer.

MacClinton

(They continue to wrestle, and MacClinton stumbles into a mud puddle. As he lunges again at MacStarr, he soils MacStarr with the mud on his clothes.)

(Enter Governor Bush[7] and Aide. They do not notice the struggling men.)

MacStarr: You mud-covered imbecile. You're right at home down here in the mud.

MacClinton: Look who's talking. You're in your element now.

(Exit MacClinton and MacStarr, fighting and wrestling.)

Governor Bush: I'm glad the friends we missed were safe arrived.

Aide: Some must go off, and yet, by these I see,
So great a day as this is cheaply bought.

Aide: MacStarr is missing, and your predecessor, MacClinton.
But they say MacStarr parted well and paid his score.
And so God be with him![8] Here comes newer comfort.

(Enter MacArmey.)

MacArmey: Hail, King! For so thou art. The time is free.
I see thee compassed with thy kingdom's pearl,
That speak my salutation in their minds;
Whose voice I desire aloud with mine.
Hail, Governor of Texas!

Aide and MacArmey: Hail, President of Bush![9]

Governor Bush: We shall not spend a large expanse of time

Act Five – Scene Seven

Before we reckon with your several loves,
And make us even with you. My friends,
Henceforth, you will be Rangers, honorary Texas Rangers.[10]
Do you want an honorary badge or a baseball bat?
Be you Rangers, the first that ever was in Washington[11]
In such an honor was named. What's more to do,
Which would be planted newly with the time,
As calling home our exiled friends abroad
That fled the snares of watchful tyranny,
Through purloined FBI files,
Producing forth the cruel ministers
Of this debaucher and his fiendish queen,
Who, as 'tis thought, by self and violent hands
Took after Monica who was running for her life;
This, and what needful else
That falls upon us, by the grace of Grace
We will perform in measure, time, and place.
So thanks to all at once, and to each one,
Whom we invite to see us sworn in at the Capitol,
And then to the big barbecue.

(*Curtain.*)

The End

Notes

Act One

Scene One

1. During the 1992 presidential campaign, Bill Clinton referred to Hillary's benefit to the country as a "buy one, get one free" deal; and Hillary liked to quote people who called the Bill-and-Hillary duality a "blue-light special."
2. Arkansas police officers testified that they had arranged countless sexual trysts for Governor Bill Clinton. One state trooper said he had solicited more than one hundred women for Governor Clinton's sexual affairs.
3. Tyson Foods had numerous chicken-processing plants in Arkansas and, in the late 1970s and early 1980s, was the state's biggest employer. In October 1978, when Bill Clinton gained the lead in the political polls in the Arkansas governor's race—which he won the following month—Hillary Clinton gave $1,000 to Tyson's outside legal counsel, and the lawyer invested the money in cattle futures. In

ten months, Hillary made $99,540 profits. The media referred to this transaction as the Cattle Futures scandal.

Scene Two

1. Kenneth Starr is a former Solicitor General of the United States and former U.S. Court of Appeals judge. Judge Starr was appointed as independent counsel to investigate the suicide death of Vince Foster, deputy White House counsel, and the Clintons' Whitewater Development real-estate investments. His role was expanded to include the investigation of perjury, suborning perjury, and obstruction of evidence relating to false testimony Clinton gave in the *Jones v. Clinton* lawsuit regarding having sexual relations with Monica Lewinsky, a young White House intern.
2. After his two federal positions, Ken Starr returned to private practice. His firm represented a tobacco company.
3. Hillary Clinton frequently referred to critics of her and Bill's abuses of power as being the result of "a vast right-wing conspiracy," rather than acknowledging their own misdeeds.
4. Judge Starr took a large pay cut to serve the country as independent counsel.
5. James "Jim" and Susan McDougal were longtime friends of the Clintons in Arkansas and were partners with Bill and Hillary in the Whitewater Development Corporation that failed. The McDougals owned Madison Guaranty Savings and Loan, which also failed, costing taxpayers more than $60 million.
6. Janet Reno was Clinton's U.S. Attorney General who initially appointed Robert Fiske as Special Counsel to investigate the allegations against Bill Clinton. Kenneth

Notes

Starr was later appointed to replace Fiske as Special Prosecutor.

7. Bill Clinton won reelection in 1996 over Republican presidential nominee Robert "Bob" Dole, a longtime U.S. Senator from Kansas and World War II hero, who had been gravely wounded in action.
8. The donkey is the traditional symbol of the Democratic Party.
9. Vince Foster was Hillary Clinton's law partner at the prestigious Rose Law Firm in Little Rock, Arkansas, and worked in the Clinton White House. He committed suicide in July 1993. White House officials blocked Washington, DC, police from searching Foster's office and briefcase for a day while Clinton's White House aides removed Whitewater documents and other incriminating documents from Foster's office.
10. Golgotha is another name for Calvary, where Jesus Christ, a truly innocent person, was crucified for our sins, so we can have forgiveness for them and a relationship with God.
11. Whitewater Development Corporation was a proposed rural real-estate development project co-owned by Bill and Hillary Clinton and Jim and Susan McDougal. Whitewater Development failed, but money from McDougals' Madison Guaranty Savings and Loan was alleged to have been used to attempt to save the project and pay tens of thousands of dollars of Governor Clinton's campaign debts.

    The collapse of Madison Guaranty Savings and Loan and more than $60 million in losses to taxpayers brought in federal investigators. Their investigation eventually led to a special prosecutor probing the President's involvement in the misuse of its funds and resulted in

MacClinton

   the convictions of numerous Clinton business partners and associates, including Governor Clinton's successor, then-Governor Jim Guy Tucker. Tucker's conviction led to the elevation of Lieutenant Governor Mike Huckabee to Governor and, later, U.S. presidential candidate.
12. The stream of women who alleged being sexually harassed by Governor Clinton, procured by Arkansas state police for his sexual satisfaction, or claimed to have had long-term sexual affairs. Paula Jones's claim was supported by her tape recordings of Clinton's phone-sex conversations with her during the course of the years-long sexual affair.
13. James Carville, Bill Clinton's 1992 campaign manager, described the long line of women claiming to have had affairs with Governor Clinton as "bimbo eruptions." Carville also said, "If you drag a hundred dollar bill through a trailer park, you never know what you will find."

Scene Three

1. During the 1992 presidential campaign, Clinton bragged about having an El Camino with Astroturf in the back, hinting it was used for impromptu sexual trysts.
2. Linda Tripp, Monica Lewinsky's confidante, reported that when Kathleen Willey left the Oval Office alleging she had just been sexually assaulted by President Clinton, Willey's clothes were disheveled and her lipstick was smeared.
3. *The Starr Report: The Official Report of the Independent Counsel's Investigation of the President* contained numerous interviews with women with whom Clinton had affairs.

Notes

4. Dick Morris assisted Governor Clinton in his gubernatorial campaigns and went to Washington to advise him early in his first term.
5. Despite clear evidence that Clinton perjured himself and obstructed the investigations, all Democrats voted against his impeachment and removal, saying, in effect, that perjury and abuse of power was permissible because, as the Democrats often said, "it was only about sex."
6. The women's tales about encounters with Clinton followed a similar pattern of being brought to the Governor by Arkansas state police troopers, having the Governor expose himself, and demanding the women satisfy him. The women told a consistent story, including Clinton's sexual demands being followed by threats if they told anyone. Several state police troopers confirmed the long-standing pattern of sexual affairs by Governor Clinton and that they were the ones who procured women for his sexual appetites.
7. "Hail to the Chief" is the musical salute to the President of the United States.
8. George Stephanopoulos was deputy campaign manager for Clinton's 1992 presidential campaign and Clinton's first communications director in the White House. In his book *All Too Human: A Political Education,* about his experiences working with Bill Clinton, he seemed appalled at reports of Clinton's wanton sexual appetite and serial affairs during the presidential campaign and in the White House.
9. In *Macbeth* Banquo was riding with Macbeth when the latter met the three witches and received the prophecy of his kingship. But the witches ignored Banquo in favor of Macbeth. Like Banquo, the ignored man lived

MacClinton

   a more normal life, not becoming king but not being destroyed either.
10. A number of Arkansas state troopers testified about repeatedly taking a series of women to meet Governor Clinton in the same room in a noted Arkansas hotel.
11. Like Macbeth relying on the three witches' half-truths that led to his destruction, so Bill Clinton risked his political life, family life, and presidency, relying on his half-truths, his lies, and the protection of his political friends and allies to conceal decades of outrageous philandering.
12. There were numerous reports of Hillary Clinton's rages at Bill for his affairs and womanizing, including one that she threw a table lamp at him in their White House bedroom. And once President Clinton had to admit a scratch on his face was not a shaving nick as reported.

Scene Four

1. The Clintons were famous in Arkansas for sitting front and center, in front of the television camera, in a Baptist church in Little Rock, where their image—that of a loving, Christian family faithfully attending church—was broadcast across the state. By the time of the presidential campaign, however, rumors about Governor Clinton's philandering were widespread across Arkansas.

Scene Five

1. The U.S. Supreme Court forced Bill Clinton to submit to sworn depositions about his involvement in Whitewater, loans from Madison Guaranty Savings and Loan, and sexual relations.

Notes

Hillary Clinton was also deposed numerous times, especially by investigators with the Resolution Trust Corporation, a U.S government agency charged with liquidating the assets of insolvent savings and loan associations in the 1980s. Investigators were specifically probing Hillary's legal work, especially for Madison Guaranty Savings and Loan. She denied directly performing any significant legal work for it. Hillary's sworn denials were later shown to be lies and perjury as confirmed by previously subpoenaed documents, the existence of which Hillary denied under oath. However, a box containing those long-subpoenaed documents was discovered years later in the highly secured private living quarters of the Clintons in the White House.

The New York Times columnist William Safire, an early Bill Clinton supporter, summarized Hillary Clinton's now decades-long penchant for lying. In his January 8, 1996, New York Times column titled "Blizzard of Lies," he wrote, "Americans of all political persuasions are coming to the sad realization that our First Lady [Hillary Clinton]—a woman of undoubted talents who was a role model for many in her generation—is a congenital liar. Drip by drip, like Whitewater torture, the case is being made that she is compelled to mislead, and to ensnare her subordinates and friends in a web of deceit."

2. The media has often promoted and repeated as truth the Clintons' lies and cover-ups. For example, national media downplayed rampant rumors in Arkansas about Clinton's philandering and parroted the Clinton line that the investigations were "just about sex" and, thus, not important. During Hillary's tenure as U.S. Secretary of State, the media derided investigations of the thirteen-hour abandonment of four Americans,

including America's ambassador to Libya, who were murdered by an organized terrorist attack in the Benghazi, Libya, consulate. Also, the media overlooked the staggering risk of American intelligence reports on private computer servers that Hillary Clinton kept in her home and in the Colorado bathroom of a couple who were doing computer support for her and through which servers Hillary conducted business as Secretary of State.

3. Hillary Clinton is noted for her cold, aloof personality. Indeed, in 2015, during her campaign for the Democratic presidential nomination, it was reported that she was counseled about how to appear nice, friendly, and relatable. Presidential candidate Barack Obama coldly appraised Hillary Clinton's aloofness in one of their 2007 debates while campaigning for the Democratic nomination: "You are likable enough, Hillary."

4. Examples of the Clintons' abuses of governmental power abound. For example, the Clinton White House improperly obtained and distributed the FBI's background checks on 900 Republicans who had been in the Reagan and Bush administrations. The Clinton White House used the FBI and other government agencies to indict and remove from his position the head of the White House travel office, so Clinton friends could be appointed to the office. The lead investigator of the Whitewater investigation was transferred from Arkansas soon after Clinton became President, temporarily halting the investigation. Even a single woman, Linda Tripp, who assisted the office of the independent counsel regarding Monica Lewinsky, was fired from her federal job on the last day of the Clinton administration. That administration received illegal campaign funds from the Communist People's Republic of China and

Notes

concomitantly vast amounts of secret technology was transferred to the communist Chinese government.

5. Hillary Clinton once told reporters she had communed with the spirit of Eleanor Roosevelt while she was in the White House.

6. In 2015 a House of Representatives committee investigating the 2012 murder of four Americans at the U.S. Consulate in Benghazi, Libya, subpoenaed emails from Hillary Clinton that "disappeared" through intentional erasing and cleaning of the personal server on which she conducted State Department business as Secretary of State. Similarly, in the months between Bill Clinton's election as President in November 1992 and his inauguration on January 20, 1993, law students at Rose Law Firm stated they worked around the clock shredding legal documents in files labeled "Whitewater." They did this despite the fact that the U.S. attorney's office in Arkansas was investigating the Whitewater Development for illegal actions, including potential bank fraud.

    Destroying or hiding subpoenaed evidence or evidence that one reasonably believes may be sought are criminal acts for which—unless you are the incoming President of the United States or the protected candidate for the Democratic presidential nomination—would lead to a quick federal indictment and prison sentence.

7. Arkansas friends had voiced an interest in running the White House travel office, which was run by a government employee, Billy Dale, who worked there for three decades. The Clinton White House sicced government investigators on Dale's office. He was indicted but quickly acquitted by a Washington DC jury. Hillary denied under oath that she was involved in the

travel-office purge, in direct contradiction to evidence from numerous White House officials. The White House's malicious persecution of Dale was so offensive that the U.S. Congress passed a bill to fully reimburse him for his legal expenses.

8. One of Hillary's first jobs as a lawyer was in 1974 on the staff of the Democratic House committee investigating President Richard Nixon's Watergate improprieties. She worked with Bernie Nussbaum, who became Bill Clinton's White House counsel. William Dixon, a member of the Democratic House committee described Hillary's single-minded focus on the impeachment of President Nixon, saying Hillary "paid no attention to the way the Constitution works in this country, the way politics works, the way Congress works, the way legal safeguards are set up" (quoted in *Hell to Pay: The Unfolding Story of Hillary Rodham Clinton* by Barbara Olson, Washington DC: Regnery Publishing, Inc., 1999, 122).

9. Many people have noted that Hillary's disinclination to admit mistakes or release subpoenaed documents is due to her recognition that Nixon's fall was due in part to his release of subpoenaed documents, rather than destroying those documents.

10. On June, 23, 1993, Lorena Bobbitt gained national attention when she cut off the penis of her husband, John Wayne Bobbitt. She was found not guilty due to insanity. Lorena's legal defense to the criminal charges resulting from her attack on her husband included allegations of John Wayne's many infidelities during their marriage. Even comedians on late-night talk shows connected the sensational Bobbitt case's allegations of infidelities to Bill Clinton's decades-long pattern of

Notes

infidelities and joked about Hillary considering giving Bill a "Bobbitt."
11. Bill Clinton built a decades' long career on his ability to seem to care about people. As he would often gush to ordinary Americans as they told him their troubles, "I feel yer pain," with a sincerity that seemed to cause women to swoon and men to vote Democratic.
12. Bill and Hillary were co-Presidents, to use the Clintons' term, from January 20, 1993, until January 20, 2001.

Scene Six

1. Senator Bob Dole has a habit of speaking in third person.
2. Senator Bob Dole was in Congress from 1961 to 1996, the last 27 years as U.S. Senator. He was Senate Majority Leader in 1995 and 1996 when the Republicans took control of the Senate after the American people threw out the Democrats due to their support of Hillarycare, the precursor of Obamacare. The Capitol building that houses Congress is on the other end of Pennsylvania Avenue from the White House.
3. Bob Dole's wife, Elizabeth, was a Republican senator. She was the first woman U.S. Senator from North Carolina. A graduate of Harvard Law School, "Libby" had previously served in President George H. W. Bush's administration as U.S. Secretary of Labor and in President Ronald Reagan's administration as Secretary of Transportation. In the latter position, she mandated the installation of brake lights above automobile trunks to reduce rear-end collisions, a lifesaving innovation that was called a "Dole light" after her. She was President of the American Red Cross before becoming a U.S. Senator.
4. Because of his near-fatal injuries in World War II, Bob Dole's right arm and shoulder were so shattered that

MacClinton

when he finally recovered after years of treatment in veterans hospitals, his right arm was frozen in place, in a slightly bent position. His right hand was atrophied and become fixed into a closed hand, virtually useless. Because of these injuries, Dole has to shake hands with his left hand.

5. Bob Dole received a Bronze Star for his service to his country in World War II. In contrast, Bill Clinton spent his college years evading and avoiding the military draft, including denying ever receiving a draft notice. However, that long-denied notice was later found and released, again showing the Clintons' consistent practice of prevarication and covering up their lies and misdeeds.

Scene Seven

1. Clinton appointed Ruth Bader Ginsburg and Stephen Breyer to the U.S. Supreme Court. He also appointed 66 judges to U.S. courts of appeals and 305 judges to U.S. district courts. There are 179 courts of appeals judges and 678 district court judges. Soon after taking office in 1993, the Clintons fired all 93 of the U.S. attorneys around the country and appointed their own people to those critical roles.

2. Sincerity is often said to be the most important quality for a politician to master. Its corollary is that once one can fake sincerity, everything is easy. Bill Clinton could summon a tear in his eye at the drop of a hat. He would lean in and look caringly into the eyes of a voter who was being crushed by life; and with the verisimilitude of concern, say, "I feel yer pain," with a twang in his voice.

3. A key component of the Clinton electoral victories were married, suburban women, who were described as "soccer moms."

Notes

4. During the 1996 presidential campaign, there were allegations that the Communist People's Republic of China was illegally funneling funds into the Clinton campaign and the Democratic National Committee.
5. On January 26, 1998, President Bill Clinton addressed the American people on television and said, "I want to say one thing to the American people. I want you to listen to me. I'm going to say this again: I did not have sexual relations with that woman, Miss Lewinsky. I never told anyone to lie, not a single time—never. These allegations are false."
6. The Clintons, supposedly ardent advocates of women's lib, have spent their careers destroying any woman who dared report that Bill Clinton had used her for his sexual satisfaction and then tossed her aside. In 1995, U.S. Senator Robert Packwood (R-Oregon) resigned from the Senate when faced with expulsion for kissing women. But the women's liberation organizations that had called loudly for Packwood's expulsion abandoned the many women whom Bill Clinton had sexually abused. Many of those organizations staunchly supported and defended Bill Clinton who had asked many women to kiss him below the belt. Evidently, for left-wing politicians and people who supposedly oppose sexual harassment of women, when it comes to kissing, what is kissed and whether it is one of their allies and friends who are accused of the sexual harassment is the issue.
7. Similarly, in 2010 the IRS levied a tax lien against Christine O'Donnell, Republican candidate for the U. S. Senate seat in Delaware, for $11,744 in back taxes and penalties immediately after she won the nomination. And, contrary to IRS rules, the IRS announced the filing of the lien for maximum political damage. However, it dismissed

the lien shortly after she lost the general election, claiming it was a mistake.

And in 2012 the IRS audited Frank VanderSloot, who was national finance committee cochairman for the Republican presidential nominee, Mitt Romney. In addition, the IRS audited his business; and the Department of Labor investigated his business. The investigation suddenly ended after Romney lost the 2012 election.

Act Two

Scene One

1. Millions of dollars of illegal campaign contributions to the Clinton campaign and the Democratic National Committee were traced to the Communist Chinese army, Communist Chinese intelligence agencies, and people closely connected to Communist Chinese leadership. After the 1996 election, large amounts of high-tech information was transferred to the Communist Chinese government.
2. Yah Lin "Charlie" Trie began as a Little Rock restaurateur but ended up bringing almost $600,000 to the President's legal defense fund, which was later returned. Trie testified before a federal grand jury investigating Communist Chinese money contributions to the Clintons. Together with John Huang and Johnny Chung, who admitted making campaign contributions on behalf of people connected with Communist Chinese, Trie was identified as being associated with the mainland Chinese influence efforts.

Notes

Scene Two

1. Monica Lewinsky often wore a black beret in the early days of her affair with Clinton to help him spot her in crowds.
2. Lewinsky testified that President Clinton was aroused by her thong underwear and frequently commented on it.
3. In one of the most disturbing images revealed in *The Starr Report: The Official Report of the Independent Counsel's Investigation of the President,* the official report of the special prosecutor's office, Monica Lewinsky stated that President Clinton inserted a cigar into her, then put the cigar in his mouth and commented on its good flavor.
4. Monica Lewinsky did not seem concerned that the Clinton team were trashing other women. After her affair with Bill Clinton ended, she was transferred from the White House. Hillary Clinton and her supporters called Monica a stalker.
5. Monica Lewinsky testified that Bill Clinton wooed her by telling her he was going to divorce Hillary and marry her.
6. Monica Lewinsky told investigators that President Clinton enjoyed talking to world leaders on the telephone while she gave him oral sex.
7. Congressman Robert Livingston was to be Newt Gingrich's successor as Speaker of the House until it was revealed he had an affair twenty years before. He resigned from Congress, calling on President Clinton to do the honorable thing and follow his example. Clinton did not.
8. Reports about Livingston's decades-past affair created a firestorm in the media.

MacClinton

Scene Three

1. The Clinton administration improperly obtained almost 900 FBI files on its perceived enemies, almost entirely Republicans, then distributed those private files to various aides and friends. This act is a violation of the FBI's strict rules for the dissemination of such sensitive information that had been obtained for government security-clearance evaluations.
2. Trent Lott (R-Mississippi) was first a Congressman, then a Senator for almost twenty years. He was Senate Majority Leader from 1996 to 2001.
3. On September 11, 2012, U.S. Ambassador Christopher Stevens and three heroic Americans were murdered during a planned, coordinated thirteen hour long terrorist assault on the U.S. Consulate Office in Benghazi, Libya.

    The U.S. Pentagon's National Military Command Center notified the Office of the Secretary of Defense Leon Panetta in Washington, DC, at 4:32 p.m soon after the attack began on Tuesday, September 11. Real-time video streams from U.S. drones, which arrived at 11:40 p.m. Benghazi time, or 5:10 p.m. Eastern Standard Time in Washington, DC, and which circled over the besieged Consulate, and allowed the White House and U.S. military leaders to watch the Ansar al-Sharia military's terrorist attack on the Americans surrounded in the Consulate.

    Although U.S. military assets, both military attack aircraft and quick-response teams like Delta Force and S.E.A.L. teams were positioned nearby in Italy and Spain and could have rescued the besieged Americans within hours, President Obama failed to send any assistance to save the brave Americans. The Ansar al Sharia militia troops burned the Consulate buildings, and murdered the U.S. Ambassador and three American defenders.

However, the Benghazi attack was less than two months before the 2012 election, so President Obama rushed, not to save the Americans besieged by a terrorist army, but rushed to protect his re-election campaign, by sending U.S. Ambassador Susan Rice onto all the mainstream news shows to promote the lie that the attack was caused by a video.

That the claim that the attack was caused by a video was known by the Obama Administration to be an absolute lie is established by a series of emails from U.S. Secretary of State Hillary Clinton to her family during the thirteen hour assault. Secretary Clinton told her family in those emails that the Obama Administration knew from the beginning of the attack in Benghazi that it was a planned military attack by an Islamist terrorist group. (<u>13 Hours: The Inside Account of What Really Happened in Benghazi</u>, by Mitchell Zukoff with the Annex Security Team, Hachett Book Group, 2014).

On January 23, 2013, testifying before the U.S. Senate committee investigating why Secretary Hillary Clinton had not provided the additional security that Ambassador Stevens had pled for in light of the tremendous risk caused by the rise of the Ansar al-Sharia in Benghazi terrorist organization and its recent attacks on other Western embassy personnel. Secretary of State Hillary Clinton breezily dismissed the brutal murder of Ambassador Stevens and the three brave American defenders when she told the Senate committee: "With all due respect, the fact is we had four dead Americans. Was it because of a protest or because a group of guys out for a walk one night who decided to kill some Americans? What difference at this point does it make?"

With all due respect, Ms. Clinton, it does make a difference, especially to the families of those four Americans murdered at the American Consulate on 9-11, 2012, and it makes a difference to all brave American troops who now know that the Obama Administration will leave them behind to die on the field of battle.

4. The impeachment process occurs in the U.S. House of Representatives. After the impeachment vote, the process moves to the U.S. Senate, which determines whether the office holder is removed from office.
5. Monica Lewinsky retained a blue dress she wore during one of her sexual trysts with Bill Clinton because several drops of Clinton's semen had dribbled onto it. As protection from the Clinton attack squad, Lewinsky kept the dress with the biological evidence of Clinton's sexual relationship with her. The blue dress, with its damning DNA evidence, established that Clinton perjured himself.
6. The office of the special counsel performed DNA testing on the deposits on Monica Lewinsky's blue dress that established the semen had come from Clinton, proving that President Clinton had lied to federal investigators, had lied in his deposition, and had lied to the American voters when he said he had not had sexual relations with Ms. Lewinsky.
7. Much like Lady Macbeth desperately attempting to wash from her murderous hands the blood of innocent King Duncan, whom she had murdered in his bed, so too Bill and Hillary Clinton surely also wished they could wash away the incriminating spots of Clinton's semen from Monica Lewinsky's soiled dress. Those spots of semen

Notes

established that Bill Clinton was, like William Safire had written about his wife, a "congenital liar."

Scene Four

1. Clinton's Vice President, Al Gore, was an advocate for strong environmental measures, which had the effect of raising costs and lowering profits for farmers.
2. Al Gore represented the United States at the 1997 Kyoto Protocol international negotiations, which severely limited the use of energy by the United States but contained few limits on energy usage by China, India, and developing countries.

    An agreement between the United States and a foreign nation is a treaty that, under Article II, Section 2 of the United States Constitution and which, prior to President Obama's Iran Nuclear Bomb treaty in 2015, required a two-thirds vote of the U.S. Senate to approve. Confronted by a catastrophic treaty that would destroy the American economy, the Senate voted 95-0 against signing the Kyoto Protocol. Senator Robert Byrd (D-West Virginia), the elder Democrat of the Senate delegation and a leader of the Ku Klux Klan in West Virginia when he was in his twenties, cosponsored the Senate resolution stating the "sense of the Senate" was for the United States not to sign the Kyoto Protocol.
3. After a stream of revelations about the sales of advanced American technology to Communist China, investigations began to center on a scientist with a Chinese surname at Los Alamos.
4. Democratic fundraiser Maria Hsia was accused of being a Chinese intelligence agent, although that charge was not proved. Johnny Chung, from Taiwan, visited the Clinton White House at least 49 times in two years,

getting photos with the Clintons and a supportive letter from Hillary Clinton. Chung donated $366,000 to the Democratic National Committee between 1994 and 1996. At least $35,000 of that money came from Lt. Colonel Liu Chaoying, daughter of a Communist Chinese general and a funnel for Communist Chinese military intelligence. In 1998 Chung was convicted of bank fraud and conspiracy to break the election law. He alleged the Chinese government tried to assassinate him three times after he gave testimony about its illegal campaign funds to the Democrats. Fundraiser John Huang, born in China, delivered $3.4 million to the Democratic National Committee, almost half of which it returned because of the questionable and illegal Chinese government sources of the money.

5. On the February 22, 1998, *The New York Times* article "Al Gore and the Temple of Cash" (a play on the movie title *Indiana Jones and the Temple of Doom*) reported how Bill Clinton's Vice President, Al Gore, attended a fundraiser in the Hsi Lai Buddhist Temple in California. He raised as much as $250,000 from Buddhist priests at an April 29, 1996, luncheon. After a year of prodding, the Justice Department finally investigated the event. Maria Hsia was charged with laundering more than $55,000 through the Temple. She was accused of being a Chinese intelligence agent when she worked with Al Gore, spanning back to fundraising for him while he was a Senator; but that charge was never proven.

The New York Times doubted Gore's "evolving" memories of that lunch, saying that if Gore was unaware of the confluence of leading Chinese intelligence agents and a quarter of a million dollars of illegal donations from Buddhist monks, "we are dealing with obliviousness of a rare order."

Notes

Attorney General Janet Reno denied requests to appoint a special prosecutor to investigate the allegations of illegal Communist Chinese campaign contributions to the Democrats and Al Gore's lies to FBI investigators about whether he knowingly attended the illegal fundraising event. Gore's aides told FBI investigators that they had told Gore about their concerns about illegal fund raising at the Buddhist temple. But in a bizarre explanation, Gore responded that he had been drinking too much tea, he went to the bathroom, and that is when the aides might have mentioned the illegality. The aides responded that if Gore had gone to the bathroom, they would have waited until he returned to continue to speak.

Nonetheless, there was no Special Prosecutor appointed by the Attorney General to investigate the alleged lies and misstatements by the Democrat Vice President.

However, in a similar vein, "Scooter" Libby, an aide to Republican Vice President Dick Cheney was investigated regarding the revelation of Valerie Plame's and Joseph Wilson's involvement in the Bush administration's investigation into whether the Iraqis were trying to buy yellowcake uranium in Niger. Special counsel Patrick Fitzgerald was quickly appointed to investigate the possible leak of Plame's undercover CIA status. Although it was known before his appointment that Plame's status had been leaked by a Democratic reporter, nonetheless Libby was tried and convicted of perjury.

6. The Red Chinese are the Communist Chinese on the mainland of China, as opposed to the Nationalist Chinese on the island of Taiwan.

MacClinton

Act Three

Scene One

1. Robert Livingston was chosen as Newt Gingrich's successor as Speaker of the House of Representatives in 1998, but he resigned from Congress after it was revealed that he had an affair many years before. That report surfaced after Larry Flynt offered one million dollars for information about sexual improprieties by Republican members of Congress.
2. The East Gate is the commonly used entrance to the White House.
3. The Supreme Court unanimously ruled against President Bill Clinton in 1997 in *Clinton v. Jones*, decreeing that a sitting U.S. President is not immune from civil litigation for actions done before becoming President and unrelated to the office of President. Clinton had tried to thwart Paula Jones's lawsuit for his sexual harassment when he was Arkansas governor. Eight justices joined the majority opinion, including Ruth Bader Ginsburg, a Clinton appointee. Associate Justice Stephen Breyer, the other Clinton appointee, filed a concurrence.
4. Representative Livingston helped lead the fight against pornography.
5. During the 1992 presidential campaign, Gennifer Flowers revealed that she and Bill Clinton had had a twelve-year affair and gave an interview in *Penthouse*. Clinton went on *60 Minutes* to deny having an affair with her. Immediately after Clinton's denial, Flowers conducted a press conference where she played tape recordings of numerous telephone conversations between her and Governor Clinton. The recordings confirmed her claim that she and President Clinton had had a years-long

Notes

sexual relationship and again demonstrated the Clintons' penchant for lying. Eight years later, Clinton admitted under oath that he had had a sexual affair with Flowers.

6. Gennifer Flowers was featured in an article in *Penthouse* after she claimed she and Bill Clinton had conducted a sexual affair in Arkansas for many years.
7. *Hustler* was Larry Flynt's "mens" magazine.
8. Flynt offered a million dollars for dirt on Republicans.
9. Janet Reno received much disgrace and contempt from the Democrats and the media for appointing a special prosecutor to investigate President Clinton on Whitewater Development and Madison Guaranty Savings and Loan issues.
10. President Bill Clinton was impeached by the House of Representatives on December 19, 1998, on one count of perjury and one count of obstruction of justice. The Senate failed to convict Clinton, as all the Democratic Senators stood in unity with their perjuring and power-abusing President.
11. On April 12, 1999, U.S. District Judge Susan Wright found Bill Clinton in contempt of court for giving 'intentionally false' testimony in Jones v. Clinton and referred Clinton to the Arkansas Supreme Court's Committee on Professional Conduct. The Arkansas Supreme Court suspended Bill Clinton's law license because President Clinton had given perjured testimony in that court case. Because of President Clinton's perjury in the Paula Jones case, on October 1, 2001, the U.S. Supreme Court suspended Bill Clinton's law license, with 40 days to contest his disbarment. On November 9, 2001, Bill Clinton resigned from the U.S. Supreme Court bar, surrendering his license rather than being disbarred for his perjury in the Paula Jones case.

MacClinton

Scene Three

1. A variant of Willie Nelson's line in the Robert Redford and Jane Fonda movie *The Electric Horseman*.
2. After the media discovered Monica and her story of an extended sexual affair in the Oval Office, the Clinton White House transferred her from the White House; and Hillary Clinton began to rant that Lewinsky was a stalker. So much for standing up for women being abused by men.
3. The dangerous "tooth" was the blue dress Monica retained as evidence of her affair with President Clinton.
4. Newt Gingrich helped draft the Republicans' Contract with America of 1994, which led to the Republicans retaking Congress. He led the Republican Congress when the Republicans balanced the budget, and he led the fight that reconfigured welfare to require recipients to work for their stipends—all over the strong objections of the Democrats and President Clinton's initial veto, which Congress overrode. Livingston had no such vast vision or accomplishments.

Scene Three

1. Livingston resigned his seat in Congress for his past affair and called on President Clinton to resign from the White House for his present affair. Clinton did not.

Act Four

Scene One

1. Newt Gingrich divorced and remarried twice.
2. A string of church arsons occurred during the Clinton administration. Though most of the churches were those

Notes

with white congregants, the Clintons and the media promoted the misleading story that the burnings were civil-rights violations. Rather than being an assault on all Christian churches, the news was reported as a series of black-church burnings.

3. El Niño and La Niña are meteorological terms that refer to cyclical heating and cooling of the Pacific Ocean, which then affect the weather across North America.
4. Al Gore and environmentalists contend that any untoward weather event—whether high wind, no wind, too much rain, or too little rain—to be absolute proof of global warming and an impending climatic Armageddon. As Gore alleged in his 2006 documentary, *An Inconvenient Truth,* the Earth is warming and land at lower levels soon will be flooded, despite the fact that the world's temperature had not risen between 1997 and August 2012 (according to an October 13, 2012, report in *Daily Mail*), another "inconvenient" truth.
5. Having defeated President George H. W. Bush in the 1992 election, Clinton was confronted with Governor George W. Bush winning the 2000 presidential election.
6. George H. W. Bush was the forty-first President of the United States.
7. George W. Bush, the son of George H. W. Bush, was the forty-third President of the United States. He was Governor of Texas when he won the 2000 election.
8. Jeb Bush, son of George H. W. Bush, and brother of George W. Bush, ran for the 2016 Republican presidential nomination. Jeb Bush was a well-regarded Governor of Florida.
9. George P. Bush, son of Jeb Bush, and grandson of President George H.W. Bush, is the elected Land Commissioner of Texas.

MacClinton

10. Ken Starr was born and raised in Vernon, Texas, along the Oklahoma border and not far from Arkansas. He attended Harding College in Arkansas for two years before transferring to George Washington University.

Scene Two

1. Judge Ken Starr's family suffered from myriad attacks on Ken's character and motives, including a whirlwind of attacks in the press, in popular media, and by late-night talk show comedians.

Scene Three

1. Kathleen Willey and her husband were strong Clinton supporters and acquaintances of Bill Clinton. Mrs. Willey went to the Oval Office to meet with President Clinton to ask him for a paying job in government in order to support her family. Linda Tripp reported that Ms. Willey came out of her meeting with Clinton badly disheveled and her lipstick smeared. Ms. Willey allegedly told her friends that Clinton had attempted to sexually assault her in the Oval Office.

    Ms. Willey has steadfastly continued her claim that President Clinton sexually assaulted her. As Ms. Willey wrote in the Foreword of Roger Stone's book, <u>The Clintons' War on Women:</u> "In 1993, I was sexually assaulted by Bill Clinton, then president of the United States, in the Oval Office. In a professional setting where I had plannned to ask him for paid employment, President Clinton put my hand on his genitals. He then proceeded to overpower me and run his hands up my skirt, over my blouse and my breasts. If not for an impending meeting for which the president was late, I might not have escaped his grasp. . . . It is my firm belief that Hillary Clinton was behind a criminal terror campaign designed to scare me into silence. As I wrote in my book, <u>Target: Caught in the Crosshairs of Bill and Hillary Clinton</u>, my children were threatened by 'detectives' hired by Hilllary. They threatened my friend's children. They took one of my cats and killed another. They left a skull on my porch. They told me I was in danger. They followed me . . . ." (<u>The Clintons' War on Women</u>, Skyhorse Publishing, 2015, p. 11-12).

2. Mrs. Willey's husband committed suicide on the day President Clinton sexually assaulted her.

3. When word reached the White House of Mrs. Willey's allegations of Bill Clinton's attempted sexual assault, the White House began a campaign of personal and character attacks against the still-grieving widow.

4. Hillary Clinton has contended since the 1990's that all the Clintons' troubles were merely the product of what she alleged was a "vast right-wing conspiracy." However, the mainstream media's support and defense of the Clintons and the media's suppression of negative reports about them suggest, in actuality, it was a vast left-wing conspiracy of support for the Clintons.

5. During the 1992 presidential campaign, the Clintons went on *60 Minutes* to rebut rumors that Bill had had a series of sexual affairs during their marriage. Hillary piously stated that she was not a stand-by-your-man woman who stays at home baking cookies, implying that if Clinton was still having affairs, she would have ended their marriage. The interview stopped Clinton's slide in the polls, leading to his election victory. Bill's philandering continued. So much for Mrs. Clinton's honor and truth-telling.

MacClinton

6. Every Democratic Senator supported Bill Clinton and voted to shield him from being removed as President after the House impeached him. So there were enough Democrats in the Senate to beat the honest men.
7. Soon after she went public about President Clinton's attempted sexual assault against her, Mrs. Willey claimed she was approached in her neighborhood by a stranger who knew her and her children by name, terrorizing her with the knowledge that the Clintons' attack machine would threaten her and her family face-to-face in a public place.
8. The mainstream media took the Clintons' side, savaging Mrs. Willey and defending the Clintons.

Act Five

Scene One

1. This dialogue foreshadows Hillary Clinton's storing State Department emails on her private computer server and then, in 2015, erasing the server's hard drive after the emails had been legally subpoenaed, in violation of a host of federal criminal laws.

    During the investigation by the Resolution Trust Corporation (RTC) into the failure of Madison Guaranty Savings and Loan and the resulting $60 million loss to the American taxpayers—including allegations that some of the money went into the Clintons' and the McDougals' Whitewater Development project—the federal investigators subpoenaed all documents related to the Whitewater Development project. Hillary Clinton swore under oath and in written depositions that she did not have any documents related to the Whitewater Development fiasco.

Notes

But years later, Carolyn Huber, a White House aide and former office manager at Hillary Clinton's Arkansas law firm, found a box containing copies of the subpoenaed documents in the President's private living quarters of the White House. The documents, many of them Hillary's personal billing records, established her long-denied but deep involvement in legal representation of Madison Guaranty Savings and Loan, which was run by the Clintons' business partner Jim McDougal. Forensic testing revealed that Hillary's fingerprints were found on the long-subpoenaed files in the hidden box.

It is significant that when the RTC, the government agency that supervised the bailout of failed savings and loans in the early 1990s, declined to file a civil lawsuit against President Bill and Hillary Clinton for their involvement in the collapse of Madison Guaranty Savings and Loan, the RTC stated that it was because it lacked the same Rose Law Firm billing documents that Hillary had hidden.

2. Monica Lewinsky told her friend at work, Linda Tripp, about her affair with Bill Clinton. Tripp tape-recorded Monica's tales of giving oral sex to President Clinton in the White House and gave the recordings to Ken Starr's office. Together with Clinton's stains on Lewinsky's blue dress, the tapes established that the President had perjured himself in his deposition when he denied the sexual affair.

3. In the tape recordings, Monica Lewinsky said that some of Bill Clinton's semen dripped from her mouth onto the blue dress she had been wearing and she kept the dress unlaundered, thus preserving Clinton's DNA evidence of that sexual encounter.

4. President Bill Clinton's semen spots on Lewinsky's unwashed blue dress were irrefutable evidence of his infidelity to his wife and perjury when he testified under oath that he had not had "sexual relations with that woman, Miss Lewinsky," a lie he also told the American people in a televised public statement.
5. Hillary Clinton has spent forty years covering up for her husband's sexual affairs and overlooking his widespread philandering.
6. Speaking with Dan Rather on *60 Minutes II*, Hillary Clinton said, "I guess I could have stayed home and baked cookies and had teas but what I decided to do was to fulfill my profession, which I entered before my husband was in public life."

Scene Two

1. The elephant is the symbol of the Republican Party.
2. Tom DeLay was a Republican Congressman from 1995 to 2003 and House Majority Leader from 2003 to 2005. A grand jury under Travis County (Texas) Democratic-led district attorney's office, which is given authority to prosecute Texas ethics violations, indicted him for money laundering. The money allegedly helped Republicans take control of the Texas House, facilitating DeLay's redistricting plan to expand Republican House representation. The conviction was overturned due to lack of evidence.

   The same district attorney's office had previously indicted Texas Republican Senator Kay Bailey Hutchison on charges of official misconduct, four months after she trounced the incumbent Democratic U.S. Senator. When the district attorney, lacking any evidence to support the indictments, was finally forced to try the case against Hutchison and the trial court required him to produce evidence supporting his indictment of Senator Hutchison, the district attorney selected a jury, then immediately dismissed the case without putting on any evidence. The trial court, as required by law, then entered a judgment of not guilty against the Republican senator.

3. Dick Armey, who has a PhD in economics, was the Republican House Majority Leader from 1995 to 2003. In 1994 he and Newt Gingrich drafted the Republicans' Contract with America, in which the Republicans promised to balance the budget, among other things. As a result of those promises, the Republicans won the House and Senate for the first time in forty years. Four years later, they enacted the first balanced budget since 1969.

4. Robert "Bob" Bennett represented Bill Clinton in the Paula Jones lawsuit, *Jones v. Clinton*. His brother, Dr. William "Bill" Bennett, served as Secretary of Education under President Ronald Reagan. Bill Bennett wrote *The Death of Outrage: Bill Clinton and the Assault on American Ideals*, a scathing book about Clinton's moral and political travesties and their corrosive influence on American decency, morality, and integrity. He also edited *The Book of Virtues*.

5. The Clinton administration improperly requested more than 900 FBI background reports and investigations on Republicans who had served in prior administrations. The FBI routinely conducts investigations and prepares these background reports on prospective White House staff and cabinet members in order to authorize security clearances. The reports contain all the information the FBI may have on individuals. The FBI Director later

said the requests were improper, were for no legitimate purposes, and violated the FBI's rules of operation.

6. George Stephanopoulos was the deputy campaign manager for Bill Clinton's 1992 presidential campaign and Clinton's first White House Communications Director. Shortly after leaving Clinton's service, he received a book contract for his memoir, *All Too Human: A Political Education,* about his time with Clinton, dealing with allegations of Clinton's numerous sexual affairs and unending cascade of lies about his countless political and personal scandals. Stephanopoulos also decried the Rose Law Firm, where Hillary was a partner, calling it "Little Rock's version of [John Grisham's] 'The Firm.'"

7. On leaving the Clinton White House, George Stephanopoulos became a political commentator for ABC News and later hosted ABC News' Sunday morning political show, *This Week*. In 2009, he became cohost of *Good Morning America*. He also served as chief anchor for ABC News. In 2014, he signed a seven-year contract extension with ABC worth $105 million.

He contributed $75,000 to the Clinton Foundation in 2012 to 2014. In 2015 he conducted a strong interview with Peter Schweizer about Schweizer's book *Clinton Cash*. The book deals with massive donations to the Clinton Foundation by foreign governments and individuals at the same time Secretary of State Hillary Clinton was making decisions that greatly benefited those countries and people. In February 2016, it was revealed the F.B.I. was opening an investigation into the possible connection between donations to the Clinton Foundation and subsequent decisions and actions by Secretary of State Hillary Clinton which benefited

Notes

those donors, just as Schweizer's book *Clinton Cash* had alleged.

Scene Three

1. President Clinton wore a gold tie for a televised press conference on August 6, 1998, the day Monica Lewinsky gave her testimony to the grand jury investigating Clinton's perjury and obstruction of justice. It was the same tie Lewinsky gave him during their affair. Later, prosecutors asked if he wore the necktie as a signal to Lewinsky that he was thinking about her during her testimony.
2. Buddy was the Clinton's dog in the White House.
3. After he retired from the U.S. Senate, Bob Dole was a spokesman for Viagra.

Scene Four

1. Henry Hyde was a Republican U.S. Congressman from Illinois in 1975 to 2007 and a member of the U.S. Navy and Navy Reserve, attaining the rank of commander. A strong supporter of the right to life, Hyde was a staunch opponent of abortion and the author of the Hyde Amendment that prevents the use of federal Medicaid funds to pay for abortions. Hyde was chairman of the House Judiciary Committee and a House leader of President Clinton's impeachment trial.
2. Newt Gingrich was Republican Speaker of the House of Representatives from 1995 to 1999. He assumed that role after the Republicans took over the House when American voters turned against the Democrats after Hillary Clinton attempted to socialize health care. Gingrich and the Republicans drafted a pledge to the American voters, Contract with America,

MacClinton

wherein the Republicans promised that if they won the House of Representatives, they would, among other things, balance the budget. After winning the House, the Republican-controlled Congress enacted welfare reform (the work requirements of which President Barack Obama overruled with an executive order) over President Clinton's strong opposition. In 1998 the Republicans passed the first balanced budget since 1969. Gingrich has a PhD in European history and was a history professor before being elected to Congress.
3. The Tidal Basin is a reservoir flowing from the Potomac River and is adjacent to the Jefferson Memorial, the FDR Memorial, and the Martin Luther King, Jr. Memorial.
4. Cherry trees lining the Tidal Basin were a gift to the United States from the people of Japan in 1912.
5. Democrats suggested that Congress censure President Clinton for perjury and obstruction of justice, rather than impeach him.

Scene Five

1. And yet, two decades later, the Clintons are still strutting across the stage, still amassing a vast fortune (they have an estimated net worth of between $100 and $200 million). Plus the Clinton Foundation has raised almost $2 billion.

Scene Seven

1. After reports of the long-term sexual affair between President Bill Clinton and 22-year-old White House intern Monica Lewinsky, Clinton publicly denied the allegations and personally denied them to his inner staff and supporters. When it was announced that DNA testing evidence confirmed that the spots on Lewinsky's

blue dress was what she had said, Clinton's sexual emissions, he admitted to his staff that the affair was true. But then he told the staff, to whom he had lied for months, that they would have to continue to soldier through with the lie. Rather than admit publicly that Clinton's statements denying the affair were outright lies, the administration continued to lie, obfuscate, and obstruct the investigation in the hope that he could survive the impeachment vote. He did.

2. President Richard Nixon resigned the presidency in face of bipartisan opposition in Congress when the Republicans joined the Democrats in calling for his removal from the office for obstruction of justice. By stark contrast, no Democratic Senator voted to remove Clinton from the Presidency despite overwhelming evidence that he had obstructed justice and committed perjury.

3. One of Bill Clinton's most effective artistic devices was his ability to mist up and cry, with a catch in his voice, at any moment. The best example is still available on the Internet. Ron Brown, Clinton's Secretary of Commerce, died in a plane crash in Croatia in 1996. As he was leaving Brown's funeral, Clinton was videoed laughing with friends until he saw the cameras and immediately teared up and began to wipe "tears" from his eyes. Unfortunately for the Clinton act, the people with whom he had been laughing did not see the cameras and continued laughing while Clinton was wiping away his fake tears.

4. On January 26, 1998, President Bill Clinton told the nation in a televised address, "I did not have sexual relations with that woman, Miss Lewinsky."

5. President Bill Clinton's defense against the perjury charge was that his statement, "there's nothing going

on between us," was truthful because at the time of his response, he was not then engaged in his sexual affair with Miss Lewinsky. As Clinton explained in classic Clintonese obfuscation, the meaning of the word *is* is indeterminate or, as Clinton phrased it, "It depends upon what the meaning of the word 'is' is."

6. Vice President Al Gore was the Democratic nominee for President in the 2000 election. He was known for his stiff, wooden debate and campaign style.
7. Texas Governor George W. Bush, the son of the forty-first President, George H. W. Bush, won the 2000 election over Bill Clinton's Vice President, Al Gore. He was inaugurated the forty-third President on January 20, 2001. However, his electoral victory was delayed by the Democrats' contest of the voting in Florida, a state Bush won by 537 votes out of millions cast. The Florida election contest led to lawsuits regarding the actions of Democratic election judges in select, heavily Democratic counties that went to the U.S. Supreme Court.

The Democratic election judges continued to change the standards for determining the "intent" of voters by the depth of indentations on the paper ballots cast, moving from recognizing the choices of voters where the ballots were fully penetrated by the stylus, then awarding Al Gore the vote if the election judge could "discern" that the ballot was "dimpled" next to Gore's name. The indefinite, changing definition of what constituted a vote for Gore led the U.S. Supreme Court to order the election judges to choose and stay with a single definition of what constituted a ballot cast for Gore.

On April 4, 2001, Mark Siebel, managing editor for *The Miami Herald*, announced that *The Miami Herald*, Knight Ridder newspapers, and *USA Today* had funded a recount of the votes in the contested Florida counties. They wanted to determine whether Bush had truly won Florida or had the Supreme Court, by stopping the manual ballot recount in those challenged counties, improperly awarded Florida and, thus, the Presidency to President Bush. After a thorough recount by the news organizations, using the Democrats' own pro-Gore standards of determining the unknowable intent of the voters, *The Miami Herald* concluded that not only had Bush legally and fairly won the election but that, as a result of the recount, his margin of victory grew from 537 votes to 1,665 votes.

8. After serving as Special Prosecutor for the President Bill Clinton investigation and impeachment trial, Kenneth Starr served as Dean of the Pepperdine School of Law. Since 2010, Mr. Starr has been President of, and in 2013 was also named Chancellor of Baylor University in Waco, Texas, where he also teaches U.S. Constitutional Law at Baylor University School of Law.

9. As Macbeth was succeeded by Malcolm, the son of Macbeth's predecessor, King Duncan whom Macbeth murdered, similarly, George W. Bush, the forty-third President and son of President George H. W. Bush, succeeded President Bill Clinton who beat President George H. W. Bush in the 1992 election.

10. Before being elected Governor of Texas by trouncing then-Governor Ann Richards (who was the mother of Cecile Richards, now president of Planned Parenthood), George W. Bush was part owner of the Texas Rangers major-league baseball team.

11. The Texas Rangers baseball team, located in Arlington, Texas, had moved from Washington, D.C., where the team had been called "the Washington Senators."

About the Author

Sam Griffith is a retired Justice on the Texas Twelfth Court of Appeals, a position to which he was elected three times, twice unopposed. As a high school senior, he worked after school each day full time in a manufacturing factory, then worked his way through college and graduate school, and through law school. Before being elected an appellate justice in 2000, he was a trial court judge and trial lawyer. He earned two legal specialization certifications from the Texas State Bar Association's Board of Legal Specialization, an achievement of less than three percent of Texas lawyers.

Outside of the court room, Judge Griffith taught U.S. Constitutional Law at universities in Iraq and China, preached through northern Iraq and South Sudan, funded twelve water wells in South Sudan, and built homes for earthquake survivors in Nepal. In addition, he cofounded a vegetable-growing ministry that was featured in a *New York Times* article and which, in five years provided more than one hundred tons of vegetables for local food banks.

Contact Information

To order additional copies of this book, please visit
www.conservativepressbooks.com
Also available on Amazon.com and BarnesandNoble.com
Or by calling toll free 1-844-2REDEEM

CPSIA information can be obtained
at www.ICGtesting.com
Printed in the USA
FSOW01n1543030516
19981FS